EMOTIONS
ANONYMOUS

ACKNOWLEDGEMENT

As members of Emotions Anonymous, we have revised the book, *Emotions Anonymous*, in order to share what we have learned about emotional recovery in our twelve-step program. We are grateful to those members who came before us for establishing this fellowship. We thank them for writing the first edition of our book, printed in 1978, which served as our guide for understanding the program. We also appreciate all those who started meetings and were there when we needed them. Without these people we would not have found this means of recovery from our emotional problems.

It is our sincere hope that this book will be useful to those unfamiliar with the Emotions Anonymous program and to others on their personal journey of emotional recovery.

EMOTIONS
ANONYMOUS

Revised Edition

Published by
Emotions Anonymous International Services
Post Office Box 4245
Saint Paul, Minnesota 55104-0245
United States of America
www.EmotionsAnonymous.org

First revised printing 1995
Index added 1996
Tenth printing 2012

Library of Congress Catalog Card Number: 95-060130
ISBN: 978-0-9607356-5-5

Preface

Emotions Anonymous (EA) was formed by a group of individuals who found a new way of life by working the twelve-step program of Alcoholics Anonymous, as adapted for people with emotional problems.

We invite you to discover, as we have, that our EA fellowship of weekly meetings is warm and friendly and that it is also important for achieving and maintaining emotional health. We use the Twelve Steps and the Twelve Traditions as guides for our meetings and for living one day at a time.

Emotions Anonymous is a non-profit organization, supported by the voluntary contributions of its members.

We thank Alcoholics Anonymous for their permission to use this program, and we thank the God of our understanding for guidance.

God grant me the serenity
To accept the things I cannot change,
Courage to change the things I can,
And wisdom to know the difference.

CONTENTS

PART I – THE PROGRAM

An Invitation 1
History of EA 7
The Hope EA Has to Offer.................................... 13
Professional Opinions.. 23
How It Works 39

PART II – PERSONAL STORIES

Come Fly With Us — *Doris* 85
At Peace — *Cassa* 92
Anxiety Got My Attention — *Bill* 95
I Did the Footwork — *Cathy*.................................. 99
No Longer a Victim — *Christina*........................... 105
Recovering From Fear — *Arlene* 109
My Life Will Be Great When — *Barb* 113
A Life of Anger — *Al* 118
Living Inside My Skin — *Linda* 123
It Was a Dark and Stormy Night — *Ken* 130
Filling the Hole in My Heart — *Miriam*................ 134
Trying to Find the Real Me — *John*...................... 139
I've Come Home — *Dian* 144
I Am a Survivor — *Jackie* 149
I Had to Accept Before I Could Recover — *Vicky*............ 153
The Tapestry — *Linda* 158
EA—I Had to Check It Out — *Tillie* 162

CONTENTS

Meetings Are For Me — *Candy* 166

There's Nothing I Can Do — *Verna* 171

No Questions Asked — *Ron* 175

I Was Afraid of My Fear — *Jerry* 179

Bipolar Disorder: A Modern Story — *Peanut* 184

No More White Knuckles — *Carol* 188

Too Much Excess Baggage — *Jack* 192

Journey Toward an Effective Life — *Kitty* 198

My Implosion — *Vivienne* 204

Thank You Higher Power! — *Bob* 207

My Accidental Blessing — *Agnes* 215

Food Was Only a Symptom — *Mary* 221

PART III — TOOLS FOR RECOVERY

Helpful Concepts 231

Just For Today 233

Slogans We Use 235

The Twelve Traditions 236

The Twelve Steps 238

The Twelve Promises 239

How to Contact Emotions Anonymous 240

Index 241

PART I

Our Program

AN INVITATION

You are not alone

Emotions Anonymous (EA) is a fellowship of people who share their experiences, feelings, strengths, weaknesses, and hopes with one another in order to solve their emotional problems and to discover a way to live at peace with unsolved problems. We come to EA to learn to live a new way of life by using the twelve-step program. Through it, we find serenity and acquire peace of mind.

Everyone is welcome in EA. All that is needed to join us is a desire to become emotionally healthy. We have discovered no one is unique in the problems or illnesses they are experiencing. The inability to cope with life can affect people of all ages and from all types of backgrounds. Emotional illness does not discriminate because of age, sex, religion, race, income, or occupation. We may have come to EA simply because life was uncomfortable and we were looking for a better way. Or, we may have been in the depths of despair, been in therapy or even hospitalized. We may have found ourselves dependent on medication, other drugs, or alcohol.

The symptoms which led us to seek help are diverse. These can include depression, anxiety, relationship or work problems, inability to cope with reality, or psychosomatic ailments. It is often the opinion of health care professionals that many physical illnesses are aggravated or caused by emotions. It is important to remember, however, that not all symptoms are caused by emotions. It is best to see a doctor to ensure your symptoms are not caused by a physical illness.

We use the Twelve Steps and Twelve Traditions of Alcoholics Anonymous, which we have adapted for people with emotional problems. We follow the Twelve Steps because they tell what people before us have done to become emotionally well. The steps are written in past tense as statements of actions already taken, attitudes already learned, and feelings already expressed – all of which have brought recovery to others. Thousands of people have gained emotional health by applying these steps in their lives.

The Twelve Steps are goals toward which we work and the measuring stick by which we estimate our progress. At first we found we did not completely understand the steps or how to apply them to our lives. Much of the thinking contained in them was totally foreign to many of us. The important thing is that we try each day to understand the steps better and to practice them in our daily lives, one day at a time. There is no right or wrong way to work this program; members practice this twelve-step program in their own individual ways.

Emotions Anonymous is supported by contributions from our members as well as from the sale of EA books and literature. No financial support is accepted from outside sources. Money is needed to maintain our program; however, no dues or fees are required in order to come to our meetings. Donations are collected at each meeting to cover expenses such as rent and literature. After group expenses are paid, the remainder is contributed to EA's International Service Center and the local intergroup to support the other services of our fellowship which carry our message of hope to others worldwide.

Because we are an anonymous organization, we identify ourselves by first names only. It does not matter to whom we are related, where we live, or where we work. Anonymity gives us the freedom to share our thoughts and feelings at meetings because what is said there is not to be repeated to anyone.

Practicing anonymity also means using only first names when representing EA in the press, on radio and television, or in any other public forum. This assures that no one member can or does speak for the entire Emotions Anonymous program. Through anonymity, the focus remains on the EA program rather than on the person sharing our message.

Emotions Anonymous is non-professional. Our meetings are not run by doctors, therapists, social workers, or any other professionals. People in these professions may attend EA meetings, but they are there for personal recovery like everyone else and not to conduct the meetings in a professional capacity. Members take turns leading the meetings because we are all equal with no one being more important than another.

At our meetings we discuss the program and how it helps us daily in our recovery. We do not discuss religion, politics, national or international issues, or other belief systems or policies. EA has no opinion on these outside issues nor on any therapy, medication, or mental health issue. It is up to individual members whether professional counseling is appropriate for them. We offer only our EA program.

Emotions Anonymous is a spiritual program; it is not a religious program. It may seem that the terms spiritual and religious are synonymous, but they are not. Religious means following specific teachings or the doctrines of established religious groups. Spiritual indicates a belief in something which is greater than oneself which can be a source of power for change in our lives. The steps suggest a belief in a power greater than ourselves, and we can define this however we want. For example, this can be the group, nature, the universe, a Higher Power, the God of our own understanding, or any entity a member may choose. The program does not tell us what we must believe; it is up to each of us to determine that for ourselves. People of many different religions as well as those of no religion are members of EA.

In EA literature, we use gender-neutral language. However, in the Twelve Steps and Twelve Traditions God is referred to in masculine terms because Alcoholics Anonymous, who granted us permission to adapt their steps and traditions to our program, views these as historic writings that should remain unchanged. EA members are free to use whatever term and gender is most helpful in developing a relationship to a power greater than themselves.

At meetings we learn that symptoms and backgrounds do not matter. We do not judge what anyone has done in the past, nor do we diagnose or give advice on personal or family matters. We take responsibility only for our own emotional recovery. We do not try to cure or change others but, instead, extend love and acceptance. Being accepted by others can be the beginning of learning to accept ourselves. As we listen to other members, we discover things about ourselves. We are amazed to hear people describe the very feelings we thought were unique in ourselves. Eventually we lose our amazement and realize how much like others we are. We no longer feel alone, and we begin to act upon the knowledge we have gained. We attempt to make changes in our lives which will bring us emotional well-being.

The program does not work overnight. It has usually taken years for us to reach the point where we are willing to seek help, and it is unrealistic to expect immediate results. At first we experience hope by observing others who were like us and who found help through Emotions Anonymous. Then, as we begin to practice the Twelve Steps, we find our lives begin to change. As we grow in the program, we experience a peace not known before.

If you are not as happy as you would like to be, or if you have tried other methods of help and still feel something is missing, we invite you to read this book. In it we share our experiences; how we once were, what we did, and how we are today after practicing the twelve-step program of Emotions Anonymous.

We invite you to attend our weekly meetings. We hope you will find them warm and friendly. We believe weekly meetings are very important for achieving and maintaining emotional health. You may find a phone number for Emotions Anonymous in your local phone book, in the support group listings in newspapers, or from community referral agencies. You may write Emotions Anonymous, International Service Center, P.O. Box 4245, St. Paul, MN 55104-0245, for assistance in locating the nearest EA group. The International Service Center can also be reached by phone at (651) 647-9712, fax at (651) 647-1593, or by e-mail at **GeneralInfo@EmotionsAnonymous.org.** Our web site located at **www.EmotionsAnonymous.org** always has current meeting information. If there is no group in your area, our staff will be happy to send you information on starting one.

We hope you will join us!

History of EA

First things first

Emotions Anonymous was started in July 1971 in St. Paul, Minnesota, by a group of people who had previously been members of another twelve-step program.

EA's roots, however, go back to October 1965 when Marion F. read a newspaper article about an organization which had adapted the twelve-step program of Alcoholics Anonymous for use in overcoming emotional problems. Marion had experienced many years of fear and panic, and this sounded like an answer for her. However, there were no groups in her area.

In February 1966 a friend asked Marion to attend an Al-Anon meeting. There she discovered people using the same Twelve Steps which she had read about in the newspaper. She continued to attend Al-Anon meetings and began to work that program.

With the encouragement of her doctor, who could see the progress she was making because of that program, Marion decided to start a group of Neurotics Anonymous (NA), the twelve-step fellowship mentioned in the newspaper article she had read. The first meeting was held on April 13, 1966, at the Merriam Park Community Center in St. Paul. Several Al-Anon members came to the first few meetings to give support. About twelve people came to that first meeting and the next week, due to a newspaper article, sixty-five people attended.

By the fall of that year a member of the first group decided to start a group in Minneapolis. Other groups spread throughout the Twin Cities area, to other locations in Minnesota, to neighboring states, and to one foreign country. Soon there were over thirty groups and a Minnesota Intergroup Association was formed. The first Neurotics Anonymous meeting in Germany was started by Walther L. and held on August 5, 1967.

In time, differences developed between these groups and the main office of Neurotics Anonymous. After a number of attempts to settle their disagreements, the Minnesota Intergroup Association voted on July 6, 1971 to disassociate itself from Neurotics Anonymous. Four days later, these intergroup members formed a Trusted Servants Temporary Committee for the purpose of forming their own twelve-step fellowship. They elected officers, chose the name Emotions Anonymous, and wrote Alcoholics Anonymous World Services, Inc. for permission to adapt and use their Twelve Steps and Twelve Traditions. Permission was granted and Articles of Incorporation for Emotions Anonymous were filed with the Minnesota Secretary of State on July 22, 1971. This new twelve-step fellowship was now officially on its way.

In August, Walther came to Minnesota and attended a meeting of the Trusted Servants Temporary Committee. Upon his return to Germany, the members of this group also disassociated from NA and joined EA on August 9, 1971.

The first trusted servants of EA learned a great deal about how A.A. operated by studying the Alcoholics Anonymous manuals. They wished to be successful so they closely followed A.A.'s way of doing things. They followed Tradition Two whereby decisions were not made by one person, but had to be done through group conscience votes. Whether in a group meeting, a committee meeting, or any other EA meeting, decisions were always to be made by a majority vote of the entire group.

That year the Trusted Servants Temporary Committee wrote bylaws and started writing literature. The first year of EA was one of new ideas, hard work, struggles, personality clashes, and growing pains.

After the bylaws were written, the membership met to ratify them and to put them into practice. This was done at the time of the first annual convention held in St. Paul on October 14, 1972. The Trusted Servants Temporary Committee was dissolved, its work having been completed. An International Service Board of Trustees was elected consisting of eleven in-town trustees, four area trustees, and seven regional trustees. The International Service Board of Trustees continues today to be the decision-making body for the business and organizational side of Emotions Anonymous.

As with most organizations, changes were inevitable. In 1975 three non-member trustees were added to the board: a pastor, a lawyer, and a member of another twelve-step group. They were chosen for their support of our program, for their various talents and backgrounds, and for the additional perspectives they would add to the decision-making process. In September 1994 the membership ratified a revised set of bylaws and reduced the size of the board to three area trustees; nine regional trustees; and three non-member trustees, an accountant, a lawyer, and a businessman. In addition, each continent may elect an international representative to serve on the board.

The primary purpose of the EA organization was originally and still is to carry the EA message of hope to people who suffer from emotional problems. It necessitated having a location where people could telephone or write for information. For those first years the office was in Marion's home, with first Marion and then other volunteers helping to answer the telephone, mail information, and keep records. For many years volunteers continued to do most of the office work for EA.

In January 1974 the office was moved and a part-time staff member was hired. EA's new location became a rented room at the Midway YMCA in St. Paul. The EA office, now known as the International

Service Center, moved to three subsequent locations as more space was needed. The paid staff has increased as well. Today EA has a full-time Executive Director, three other full-time and one part-time employees.

Since this is a fellowship run by members, for members, it has always been necessary for those making decisions for EA to maintain communication with the membership. In April 1972 a decision was made by the Board of Trustees to have an *International Services Bulletin* published four times a year and mailed out to groups. This publication continues to be sent to all registered EA groups as a communication between the board, the International Service Center, and registered groups. Since EA is an organization with no membership lists, the success of this communication rests with each EA group providing the Service Center with the address of its current contact person who then shares the Services Bulletin with the group.

In 1976 the first annual report was printed as a way to keep the membership better informed of the activities and accomplishments of the board during the previous year. This continues to be published and made available to members.

As EA groups continued to grow and spread throughout the world, a world directory was established in 1973. This publication lists meeting locations and information about groups worldwide. It is used by those looking for a group in their area as well as by members who might be moving or traveling to another area. It is important for people to be able to find EA meetings. The success and accuracy of this directory is dependent upon groups sending updated meeting infor-mation to the International Service Center.

The writing of literature was another important activity started by the first EA members. It has been done by EA members working on a volunteer basis. One of the first pieces of literature was the yellow pamphlet, first published in August 1971. By 1978 this pamphlet had been published in Braille and in a large-print edition for the visually impaired. EA has over fifty pieces of literature, some translated into as many as seventeen different languages.

In January 1972 the first issue of the monthly magazine *Carrying The EA Message* was published. It continues to be EA's "meeting in print," publishing what members write about their EA experiences. The first subscription price was $3.00 per year, and five hundred copies were printed. Currently there are 900 subscriptions.

Perhaps EA's biggest literature accomplishment was the publication of the book *Emotions Anonymous* in the fall of 1978. The original idea was to write a booklet which was expected to be completed within six months. Approximately ten members worked diligently combining ideas, writing, and rewriting. The book began to come together after two or three drafts, and, finally, after two and one-half years it was completed. At that time a typesetting machine was rented and three or four members did the typesetting.

A giant leap of faith was taken for the first printing of the book; 4,000 copies were ordered with borrowed money. It was not known if EA had 4,000 members who would buy the book; however, to date over 225,000 copies have been sold. The book is also available on audio cassette and in 1982 a German translation of the book was copyrighted. The first major revision of the book was completed in 1995.

Our daily EA meditation book, *Today,* was released in November 1987. So far 55,000 copies have been sold. Again, it was done with a few volunteers working steadily for many months. Meditations were sought from all members, but the primary work of editing and writing was done by a small non-professional committee.

The EA emblem, the letters *EA* printed in Old English script surrounded by two circles, was adopted on January 16, 1972. The circles symbolize the bond of EA members – together, equal, and never ending. This emblem is registered as EA's trademark with the United States Patent and Trademark Office.*

---

*The current logo of a bird in flight within a circle, portraying the freedom we have found in recovery, was created for the cover of the revised EA book in 1995.

Our medallion was created by members and first became available in July 1992. It has the EA emblem on one side and the Serenity Prayer on the other. A portion of the medallion's circle is flat to symbolize that our recovery is ongoing, never completed nor perfect.

The first EA International Convention was held in 1972 and conventions have been held annually ever since. The Twin Cities hosted the convention each year until 1986 when it was held in Phoenix, Arizona. Since then other cities have volunteered to be the host. The first international convention outside of the United States was held in Montreal, Québec, Canada in 1990. The first EA International Convention in Europe will be held in Germany in 1996.

The Happiness Clubs were formed in 1972. By 1974 the name was changed to Children's EA (CEA) and Youth EA (YEA). Only a few of these groups exist today.

Loners EA (LEA)* was established in 1971 but did not really become active until 1976. The purpose of LEA is to bring the Emotions Anonymous program to people who are unable to attend regular EA meetings either because there is no group in their area or because they are handicapped, housebound, or incarcerated and cannot get to a meeting. In LEA the EA program is shared through correspondence.

Emotions Anonymous has continued its growth much as it did in the beginning. Someone reads or hears about this twelve-step program which can help with emotional problems, and the person feels this could benefit him or her. Other twelve-step members have also helped get EA groups started. EA members move to new locations and start groups. LEA members start groups as they are able. As this book goes to print there are over 1,300 Emotions Anonymous groups in thirty-nine countries. The message of hope and recovery from emotional illness, begun in 1971, remains strong today.

---

*The LEA program was disbanded in 1998.

The Hope EA Has to Offer

Know yourself – be honest

Emotional illness can cripple us mentally, physically, and spiritually. It has no respect for intelligence, education, wealth, or social status. It affects not only ourselves but those who live with us and love us. This illness becomes a family illness.

When we are in the midst of emotional illness, it is hard to realize its enormity. We can understand and assess its vastness after we see the changes we and others have made with the help of the Emotions Anonymous twelve-step program.

Let us look at ourselves and at the help Emotions Anonymous has to offer. Let us see what we can do today to move toward emotional health and happiness.

The Illness

It is sometimes hard for us to realize how healthy or sick we are. In our search for self-worth and identity, we may have unknowingly set unrealistic ideals and goals for ourselves. Because our ideals are too high and we can never live up to these unrealistic expectations, our sense of self-worth is low. How can we but fail? Some of these statements might describe us:

- We want no conflict, but we still have conflict.

- We want life to be perfect here and now, but it is far from perfect.

- We want to have constant pleasure, but we have pain.

- We so much want to succeed in everything we do that, when we fail in one area, we reject all our actions and ourselves as well.

- We become very fearful.

- We try to impress other people by being someone we are not, by being phony.

- We find ourselves being resentful toward other people and life in general.

- We become experts at manipulating people.

- We become extremely self-centered.

Many of these things happen gradually, and we may not even be aware of their presence and influence in our lives. Emotional illness can be progressive and chronic. If it is not faced and dealt with, it can lead to physical illness, illness brought on by our emotions. In the extreme, we might end up in a mental institution or commit suicide.

Our physical well-being is affected by our thoughts, attitudes, and emotions. Some of us have tried to avoid getting help for our emotional problems by questioning whether we have a physical illness, a mental illness, or a spiritual illness. Body, mind, and spirit make up our total human self. Each is an integral part of us and each is influenced by the others. We really cannot divide ourselves as human beings.

In the Emotions Anonymous program, we do not analyze emotional illness. We do not label and categorize everything. We stop using our feelings of uniqueness as an excuse. We stop comparing ourselves with others. We stop blaming ourselves and others. We stop feeling sorry for ourselves, being defiant, and denying our illness. We stop making excuses and trying to convince ourselves we are different from others. These kinds of behaviors prevent us from being honest. The only purpose they serve is to perpetuate our illness. We can get help in Emotions Anonymous if we really want to be well.

We keep ourselves from becoming well; no one else does. It is our own responsibility to become well. Only when we choose to act on this responsibility will we gain the ability to recover our emotional health. If we take responsibility, we can put our past behind us and start anew, living one day at a time; but it takes conscious effort on our part. At first it may not be easy, but it is possible. We need only to begin today.

THE NATURE OF THE HUMAN MIND

While we cannot fully understand the workings of the human mind, we know it is influenced by everything we see, hear, smell, taste, and feel. Many actions we do everyday become habits and are done automatically. For the most part this is good; otherwise, we would have to learn reading, walking, eating, and many other things again and again.

Along with habits of action, we also develop habits of thought. Our thought patterns help form our attitudes toward life. These attitudes have the potential to make us well or sick, happy or miserable. It all depends on how we choose to think. Here are some questions to consider:

- Is my cup half-full or half-empty?
- Is a failure someone who does not succeed, or someone who never tries?
- Do I feel I can do something today to help myself?
- Am I able to forgive and forget injuries against me?
- Do I need other people?
- If something is worth doing, is it worth doing even if not done perfectly?
- Am I able to see the good in myself?
- Is happiness a matter of chance?
- Do I think turning to a Higher Power can help me?
- Are my emotional problems too unique to be helped?
- Am I too old to change?

• Who is responsible for my feelings?

What thought patterns do you follow? Do your answers to these questions leave the door open for growth? Do they allow you to develop to your fullest potential? If so, this indicates a positive outlook.

With a positive outlook we know we can have feelings of self-worth. We can be happy in spite of problems. We can have energy to do our daily tasks. We can feel useful; we feel we belong. We are able to adjust to life even if life does not measure up to our expectations. Peace of mind can be ours even when we are faced with difficulties. We can have a purpose to our lives; we can radiate warmth and love. We can be optimistic and accept ourselves and others.

If, on the other hand, our answers indicate a rejection of self, criticism of others, feelings of hopelessness, or a defeatist attitude, then they reflect negative thinking on our part. We may have symptoms such as anxiety, panic, abnormal fears, guilt, depression, self-pity, remorse, worry, insomnia, tension, loneliness, withdrawal, boredom, fatigue, or despair. We may experience compulsive behaviors, obsessive thoughts, suicidal or homicidal tendencies, psychosomatic and physical illnesses. If we are experiencing any of these symptoms, we must change our thought patterns or we likely will stay sick.

In the ordinary course of a day a great many thoughts pass through our minds. Naturally, some of them may be negative. It is not the occasional negative thought which causes us trouble. It is when we dwell on it, deny it, or feel guilty about it that it grows into a problem.

When we first developed our negative attitudes, we did so to protect ourselves from the pain of being rejected by others or ourselves. We chose our behaviors and attitudes to escape from reality and from the responsibility we have for ourselves and our actions. These attitudes seemed to help us for a time, but, as we built negative thought after negative thought, we became engulfed in such painful symptoms that we did not know where to turn.

Some of us sought help but could not accept the help which was offered. We may have wanted independence and hated ourselves for the dependence we felt. We may have felt too dependent on others and isolated ourselves. What we needed was interdependence with people in healthy sharing relationships. We compared ourselves with everyone; therefore, we felt inferior or superior instead of recognizing the common humanity we all share.

Our symptoms allowed us to avoid the reality of today, the reality we could not seem to face. Little did we realize that reality is heaven compared to the hell we live in with our symptoms.

AWARENESS

We finally come to realize our true state of emotional health and to say, "I have to get well. I can't stand living like this any longer. If I don't get well I'm going to lose everything — my family, my friends, my job, my peace of mind. I'm hurting myself and everyone with whom I come in contact."

Intellectually we may understand this dilemma, but, in our illness, we build up such a pattern of negative thoughts and attitudes toward life that change cannot come overnight. Responding inadequately to emotional situations has been a habit too long. Our intellect says, "I want to get well and stay well." Our emotions say, "I don't want to let go of my old attitudes and behaviors. These are all I know, and I am afraid of change, afraid of the unknown."

Before we can be well, we must realize we are not meant to be perfect for only God is perfect. We are meant to be perfectly human, and that means to be ourselves. Admittedly, we see many faults in ourselves, but we also discover many good qualities we never knew we had. Being ourselves may mean we have to change. We are always growing and discovering a little more about ourselves. There is joy and satisfaction in this discovery.

Having emotional problems should cause no more guilt than having cancer or heart disease. The guilt comes when we know we are sick, but we reject the help available. The question then is, "Do I want to get well more than I want to stay sick?" We must all answer this question for ourselves.

What can we do about our illness, about the enormity of it? Until we accept the fact of our illness, we cannot take the necessary steps to get well.

MOVING IN THE RIGHT DIRECTION

The twelve-step program of Emotions Anonymous is the answer to our problems. The first step of the Twelve Steps is to admit we are powerless over our emotions and that we are no longer able to manage our lives. We admit this on both an intellectual level and an emotional or gut level. This first step may not be easy.

By admitting we are powerless over our emotions and that our lives are unmanageable, we admit we are not self-sufficient. Are we too self-centered or self-important to make such an admission? If we want to be well, we must admit some power in the universe is greater than we are. We must become willing to turn our wills and lives over to the care of a Higher Power. This surrender is necessary if we want to get well. Fight as we might, this is one place where surrender brings true victory.

The Emotions Anonymous program is a daily living program. We do not merely join it. We try to live it — all Twelve Steps of it. We find it works. It can work for anyone who is honest with himself or herself.

EA is a program of honesty. By being honest with ourselves, we can learn to live peacefully with unsolved problems. This is serenity. As we apply this program, we find we become free, free at last to be ourselves. If we want to be well, we will learn the Twelve Steps and use them. EA is our chance to learn how to live. If we stay sick, we have no one to blame but ourselves.

By being patient with ourselves, we can become happier than we ever dreamed was possible. The more we are able to share our strengths, hopes, and imperfections, the more we can grow.

It is in the third step that we make a decision to turn our will and our lives over to the care of our Higher Power. Making the decision is the difficult part here, but it can be done if we work the program. No one can do it for us. We have to let go of our old ways of self-dependency.

We find hope as we attend EA meetings and meet other people who have found help by working this twelve-step program. A chance to be well is something some of us did not know was possible. As we attend our weekly meetings we no longer feel alone. At last we feel we belong somewhere. We are among people who understand.

The love and acceptance we experience in the group help us to accept ourselves. When others accept us as we are, we can more readily accept ourselves. We are then free to change.

Acceptance does not necessarily mean we will like who we are. Nor does acceptance mean we will stay as we are. Acceptance means admitting who we are at this moment and realizing we are powerless to change ourselves by willpower alone. Acceptance means being realistic about ourselves and saying what we really feel, instead of what we think we should feel or what society says we should feel. When others accept our feelings without trying to analyze them or judge them, we find the courage to be more honest about ourselves. In this atmosphere we do indeed grow.

As we grow, we experience the pain of healing since there is pain connected with recovery from every illness, whether physical or emotional. This healing pain is a sign of our opening up to life and self; it is a feeling of newness, of discovery. We find the rewards of an enriched life to be greater than the pain. If we heal, we will grow. If we do not, we will surely die, at least inside. As we grow, we become the unique people we are capable of being.

With the help of the Twelve Steps, we find a new way of life. With the acceptance and encouragement of the friends we make in the program, we learn to love and accept ourselves and others. With the help of a Higher Power, we find the serenity to accept what we cannot change, the courage to change what we can, and the wisdom to know the difference. With the help of the Twelve Steps, our new friends, and our Higher Power, we find ourselves and the reason for our existence. The choice is ours.

EMOTIONAL ILLNESS AND RECOVERY

Below is shown the progression of symptoms that many people may experience when in the downward cycle of emotional illness or in the upward cycle of emotional recovery. We may not all experience each symptom nor follow this exact order, and this list is not meant to be all-inclusive. Also, everyone will sink to a different depth before admitting defeat and becoming ready to accept help, this we call our emotional bottom. We can start upward toward recovery from our own emotional bottom when we truly accept the help which the EA twelve-step program offers us.

Most of us want instant recovery, but that is not possible. As with any illness, recovery needs proper treatment and care, and the time for that to work. However, often our emotional recovery will be much faster than time spent getting sick. We need only be honest, open minded, and willing to work at our recovery.

DOWNWARD CYCLE OF EMOTIONAL ILLNESS

- I have minor difficulties.
- I feel sad.
- I have more and more problems.
- I have disagreements with family and friends.
- I feel worried and anxious.
- I am irritable.
- I indulge in excessive daydreaming.
- I feel guilty.
- I feel depressed.
- I have psychosomatic ailments.
- I am losing interest in activities.
- I feel indifferent about most things.
- I make excuses.
- I try a change of location.
- I blame other people and situations.

- I feel inferior.
- I withdraw and avoid people.
- I develop chronic depression.
- I am unable to function.
- I feel extremely lonely.
- I am preoccupied with myself and my problems.
- I am unable to concentrate.
- I make varied and frustrating attempts to get help.
- I am afraid of living and of dying.
- I have an irrational but overwhelming fear.
- I feel panic and terror.
- I abuse drugs.
- I can no longer rely on my alibi system.
- I feel I am a failure.
- I consider suicide.
- I am in complete despair.

UPWARD CYCLE OF EMOTIONAL RECOVERY

- I am at my emotional bottom.
- I admit complete defeat.
- I have an honest desire to get well.
- I find the fellowship of Emotions Anonymous.
- I feel hopeful.
- I accept help and find some relief.
- I learn emotional illness can be relieved.
- I find relief from tension.
- I attend EA meetings regularly.
- I feel optimistic.
- I benefit from the shared experience of the program.
- I work the Twelve Steps.

- I meet recovering people who were formerly ill.
- I increase my faith in a Higher Power.
- I learn new attitudes, feelings, and values.
- I seek help with my fourth-step inventory.
- I can laugh again.
- I am not as fearful.
- I gain self-respect and begin to like myself.
- I am grateful.
- I am able to accept reality.
- I am happier.
- I accept my responsibilities.
- I feel a sense of well-being.
- I am able to love again.
- I have more faith and courage.
- I find life becomes smoother.
- I know the joy of living.
- I understand serenity and peace of mind.

Professional Opinions

Look for the good

Over the years, Emotions Anonymous has had good relations with medical doctors, psychiatrists, psychologists, social workers, counselors, clergy, and many other professionals. Many of them refer their patients, clients, or parishioners to this fellowship.

Perhaps you are doubtful about how a non-professional organization like Emotions Anonymous can help members become well emotionally. You may be interested in the opinions of several professionals who have observed the suffering of some of our members and have witnessed their recovery and growth through this program. This chapter contains endorsements from such professionals, and in many cases, their opinions as to why EA works.

Medical Professionals
From a doctor:

How prophetic were the words written as the citation which accompanied the Lasker Award when it was presented to Alcoholics Anonymous in 1951 by the American Public Health Association. The citation read in part, "Historians may one day recognize Alcoholics Anonymous to have been a great venture in social pioneering which forged a new instrument for social action in a new therapy based on the kinship of man's common suffering; one having a vast potential for the myriad other ills of mankind."

We also have Emotions Anonymous which opens the doorway of the Twelve Steps of recovery to the legions of persons who suffer with emotional illness. This twelve-step program suggests to the emotionally ill person: Fear no more. Turn your problems over. Know yourself, forgive yourself, change yourself, and make amends. Review your life daily; meditate. Carry the message to others with emotional ills and practice these principles in all your affairs.

Is this successful? You bet! Where there is a desire to rid oneself of the fears, anxieties, and depressions which are making one's life unmanageable and willingness to follow this program one day at a time, there is seldom failure.

I have heard many success stories from those who follow this program. Some were too fearful to leave their homes, others were on the verge of self-destruction, and others suffered from fits of anger and the emotional destruction from alcoholism. They learned that they need fear no more; that help was at hand and, indeed, it is through a Higher Power and the fellowship of Emotions Anonymous.

I am quite convinced that the principles of the twelve-step program for recovery, as begun by Bill Wilson and Dr. Bob, are indeed divinely inspired principles, that in some mystical way (similar to the way in which the authors of the Bible were inspired) they were themselves inspired in a creation of the Twelve Steps to recovery.

The world has profited from what was begun in Akron, Ohio, in 1935 when Bob and Bill first met. The twelve-step program of recovery has been applied to the emotional ills of mankind by the members of Emotions Anonymous. Their numerous stories of successful recovery are testimony to the validity of this program.

M.J. Wegleitner, M.D.
El Paso, Texas (1978)

*   *   *   *   *

From a doctor:

I have been a practicing physician for thirty years. As I entered into clinical practice, became an educator of medical students, and continued research, I learned the things not taught to me in medical school. I saw patients with chronic illnesses, and they taught me how much some people cherish life in all its different limitations and pains. They taught me human beings can adapt to life and accept limitations. They also made me realize that different problems could not be isolated from each other as if they did not interact. I could not neatly divide my patients' problems into social, physical, and psychological and pretend these issues were not somehow interdependent. They taught me I could not neatly separate body, mind, and spirit and claim I was only going to look after bodies. I learned that illness was not a mere biologic problem and correction of the biologic problem was only a portion of the solution.

There is no doubt in my mind today that the twelve-step mutual help programs like Emotions Anonymous, practiced properly, fill a gap that exists in health care today. Medicine and psychology have grown, but much of the growth has been without the proper spirit, without the humility we need to stay connected with our fellow men and women. Medicine and psychology have many of the tools that may promote healing, but the power actually doing the healing is beyond ordinary medicine. That power, that positive, creative energy that brings about change for the better is what spirituality is all about. Inserting our plug into the right socket to access that power is what the twelve-step program of recovery is about. Life is a journey toward wholeness and integration of body, mind, and spirit. The triumph of life is to overcome the resentment, fear, guilt, and shame that causes so much soul pain and isolation using the healing power that we have stored within us together with the healing power available from a recovering community like EA around us. The joy of life is to maintain that conscious contact of the Creator within us, a conscious contact with the Creator outside of us, and to live in the knowledge that both creative energies exist and actively guide us to a higher consciousness of the spiritual dimension of human beings.

Some of those who read this book may have a biologic illness and need the psychologic and spiritual support available in the program described on these pages in addition to the appropriate medicine and therapy. Some of you may have a psychologic disorder and will need healthy biologic care of nutrition, rest and exercise, psychotherapy, and the spiritual support of this program. And some may be damaged mainly in spirit. You will find the spiritual healing you require through practicing the steps and receiving the healing love and acceptance of supportive groups of EA.

Regardless of whether your dis-ease originated in body, mind or spirit, the universal healing energy available to us all may benefit you if you have the humility to be honest and ask for what you need. It is the birthright of us all to experience the healing, loving presence of a Creator through our fellow men and women. It is also our responsibility to be that healing, loving presence of a Creator to our fellow men and women. Learn from this book and use your own experience, strength, and hope with the wisdom inspired in you by your Higher Power. The energy consumed by fear, anger, guilt, and shame will be transformed into the life-giving energy of hope, acceptance, forgiveness, and self-esteem.

Dr. Bill Jacyk, M.D., F.R.C.P.
Associate Professor
University of Manitoba
Winnipeg, Manitoba (1995)

MENTAL HEALTH PROFESSIONALS
From a clinical social worker:

It is with enthusiasm that I make an endorsement of Emotions Anonymous. I am a clinical social worker who sits with people as they examine their lives in an attempt to function more comfortably. I facilitate their exploration of past experiences to learn where wounding happened and what the consequences have been. Once this is brought to light, people get the opportunity to exercise choice in whether or not the present and future are going to be like the past. New behaviors are possible in all relationships, including with the self, with intimate others, with friends, in the work place, and in the most casual encounters.

It is necessary to have a place to try on and practice these new behaviors. This is one of the most important ways that EA and psychotherapy work hand in hand.

Psychotherapy usually happens in individual sessions. Shame can be talked about and even witnessed in the one-to-one interaction; however, shame is best confronted in a group situation and particularly in a group of peers. EA provides this in a unique way. In one-on-one psychotherapy or in group therapy, the presence of a therapist (often one who is paid) creates roles and the context of leader and follower(s). Feedback from the leader can carry new shame in this very attempt to dispel shame. EA is leaderless and feedback occurs in a circle in which all are equal. Shame is healed.

The Twelve Steps of EA (or any twelve-step group) offer another pathway out of shame. Shame is that pervasive sense of being bad, a mistake; it feels like there is no way out of shame. Guilt, another learned emotion, offers a way out as it is about a specific way in which one violated a value or belief. The way out of guilt commonly used is through making apology and taking responsibility. The fourth through eleventh steps of EA guide persons in changing shame into guilt, and then into using the ordinary way out via the amends process.

Another way that I have found EA attendance to support my clients in their recovery is through the acceptance the group members offer one another. Most people who feel powerless over their emotions have never experienced unconditional love. To receive this, especially in a forum of being listened to, is very healing. It is experienced as the kind of nurturance people need in order to thrive. This process also provides another tool for healing shame as EA members can speak the unspeakable and find unwavering acceptance. Often they find sameness with others which removes the sense of isolation and differentness that so often accompanies emotional pain.

The above-described processes teach, in a supportive context, that emotions are manageable and, in fact, are being managed. In conjunction with psychotherapy, I have seen EA attendance turn lives around. Keep up the good work!

Karen N. Miller, ACSW, BCD & CSW-PIP
Clinical Social Worker
Rapid City, South Dakota (1995)

*　*　*　*　*

From a psychiatrist:

Emotions Anonymous is an excellent organization. Many of my patients, over the years, have benefited greatly from the support of Emotions Anonymous.

Emotions Anonymous fills a very special niche in the continuum of treatment. Along with other self-help groups, EA is deserving of our recognition and gratitude.

David J. Olen, M.D.
Psychiatrist
Bloomfield Hills, Michigan (1995)

*　*　*　*　*

From a psychiatrist:

I have been aware of Emotions Anonymous for many years and welcome the opportunity to endorse this very worthwhile self-help organization. The book, Emotions Anonymous, would be very beneficial for countless thousands of people who do suffer from various types of emotional problems. It is my opinion that Emotions Anonymous plays an important role in the overall treatment of people with emotional problems. The success of

Alcoholics Anonymous could very easily be equaled by Emotions Anonymous as the years go on.

It is with great pleasure that I would like to recommend Emotions Anonymous to anyone with emotional problems. I believe that it is a very excellent self-help group. I have no hesitations at all in referring my psychiatric patients there, and I do believe one of the big answers to treatment of emotional problems is through self-help groups like Emotions Anonymous.

James T. Garvey, M.D.
The Minneapolis Clinic of
Psychiatry and Neurology, Ltd.
Minneapolis, Minnesota (1978)

*   *   *   *   *

From a chemical dependency therapist:

As long as there are human beings on this earth, they will experience difficulty adjusting to the constant change taking place daily within and around themselves. This is not a profound statement, just a simple observation of people and life. This is an observation all of us can make if we just get our minds off ourselves and our own problems long enough to take a look around us.

As I work with people and hear their problems on a daily basis, several messages constantly come across to me. "My problem is worse than anyone's problem," "No one has ever had to go through what I'm going through," or "No one can help me, I just know it."

These are not unique statements from mentally ill people, but simply statements and thoughts that go through all of our minds at one time or another. Before we can begin to solve our emotional problems, we need to get over one of the biggest hurdles — lack of self-confidence. Once this is achieved, motivation will set in.

Emotions Anonymous is an organization which can help people to overcome the hurdles of self-doubt and despair which accompany our emotional unrest. EA accomplishes this task in ways that professionals cannot.

1. EA groups are not conducted by professionals in the mental health or medical field. If this does occur, it is because the individual is a member of EA and it may be his or her turn to conduct the meeting.

2. EA offers its members a program of recovery which includes the support of other people experiencing similar problems. This, I feel, helps remove the fear of change.

3. The Twelve Steps, which members follow on their road to recovery, gives them insight and direction into the problem-solving process.

4. EA helps the individual work on four important areas of his or her life, which I feel is the downfall of most other therapies which have been used in the past and are still being used to a great extent today. EA helps the individual become aware of the physical, psychological, social, and spiritual aspects of one's life and, therefore, promotes more uniform growth within the individual.

I strongly recommend Emotions Anonymous to my clients and friends who have difficulty dealing effectively with their emotions. I have also found EA to be a very beneficial referral for my alcoholic and drug addicted clients along with their regular A.A. or NA attendance.

EA is a God-sent program which can help us complicated people deal more realistically with our emotional upheavals. I need not, nor can I, say any more on the effects EA has had on many individuals' lives. Its track record, like A.A.'s, speaks for itself.

David P. Decker
Senior Chemical Dependency Therapist
Dakota County Mental Health Center
South St. Paul, Minnesota (1978)

*   *   *   *   *

From a therapist:

Emotions Anonymous has held meetings in our Guest Home, a residential facility for the chronically mentally ill, for two years.

As the supplemental rates program director, I have noticed the residents who attend weekly EA meetings have been able to open up, discuss problems, understand their emotions better and help others. Residents look forward to the weekly meetings and have been more productive in their daily lives. They relate with other members and several have become secretaries of the group.

Emotions Anonymous is a very important part of recovery for the residents at our facility.

Tara L. Eisner, Ph.D.
Marriage, Family, Child Therapist
Encino, California (1995)

*   *   *   *   *

RELIGIOUS PROFESSIONALS
From a minister:

I am honoured and pleased to be invited to write a statement of endorsement and support of the Emotions Anonymous program. It might be better called the "EA experience" and the "EA way of life."

I personally have been enriched from my involvement in Alcoholics Anonymous, Overeaters Anonymous, and, especially, Emotions Anonymous. As a guest speaker at an annual EA meeting, I found I was among friends and family — that I had come home to a caring community where one could let down the walls of deception (self and other) and be honest about one's own feelings — the feelings of depression and profound sadness that are part of the experience of every honest person. It is just a question of degree.

I find medical labels to be, in the main, rather dehumanizing and restrictive. Emotional and mental dis-ease is just that — a dis-ease, a lack of a feeling of ease and peace (serenity) and a lack of wholeness. Basically, it is a spiritual experience. Now don't get me wrong, I said spiritual, not religious.

My experience as a clergyperson for over twenty-five years, and as a person soon to be fifty, is that many people who show up at EA meetings have had bad experiences with organized religion. We are still thirsting for the spiritual water that will refresh the soul or spirit. I received a message once during a four-day fast in the Native Spiritual way. The message was "Religions divide, spirituality unites." By following the EA way of living, each day at a time, one begins to discover some clues to the question that is ultimately pure mystery and a growing sense of oneness develops.

The spirit of love, kindness, acceptance, forgiveness, respect, and equality may be found in some formal religious systems, but my experience is that the most likely place to find those spiritual qualities is in an EA circle of healing and sharing. As stories are told, we make connections with our own experience and discover we are not alone and there is hope. There is a rainbow through the storm and peace beyond the pain.

I have had the honour of sharing in many fifth steps, and I continue to be amazed at the opportunity there is to let go of old baggage when one shares the hurts, fears, and resentments of the heart with another person who can be trusted to keep a confidence.

> Whenever stories of the heart
> Are shared in Healing Circles,
> Then it is in honesty
> That we are given strength.
> Whenever two or more will share
> Experience of the spirit,
> We know the wonder of a love
> And peace that knows no length.

The sharing which goes on in EA groups can help heal wounded hearts and cause saddened souls to sing again with delight and provoke wearied spirits to dance.

I encourage and invite you to share in this spiritual search of serenity. And may you know blessings in the Sacred Circle of compassionate friends.

> What is success
> If not a contented heart;
> What is satisfaction

If not a spirit of serenity;
What is peace
If not the strength
To face life's obstacles with faith,
And to greet life's opportunities
With courage and festivity.

Reverend John Wesley Oldham
United Church of Canada
Winnipeg, Manitoba (1995)

*　*　*　*　*

From a Lutheran minister:

After many years of acquaintance with the EA way of life and many visits with persons who are living that life one day at a time, I am pleased to give the twelve-step way of life my hearty endorsement. It is, in my belief and experience, a profound spiritual, if not explicitly religious, expression of the way we are all created to live.

As persons created to live with trust in a caring Creator and with concern for our fellow creatures, we find in the Twelve Steps a way of life which leads us out of futile self-preoccupation and into a living adventure of self-surrender, self-forgetfulness, and self-giving. As we lose our lives in this venture of trust and love, we find new strength and purpose for living and experience a joy which seems possible in no other way.

We, at University Lutheran Church of Hope, are grateful that an EA group meets weekly in our building, and as a pastor, I find myself frequently encouraging persons to attend the meetings and to live the EA way of life.

May this book further extend the healing influence of EA that others, too, may receive and share its gifts of hope, meaning, and joy.

Pastor Lowell O. Erdahl
University Lutheran Church of Hope
Minneapolis, Minnesota (1978)

*　*　*　*　*

From a priest:

It is with a deep feeling of gratitude that I share these few thoughts with those who are striving for personal betterment in their relationship with self, fellow human beings, and God as they understand Him.

The basic steps of this program offer guidelines for real renewal of physical and mental well-being. It further offers opportunity for spiritual growth and serenity of spirit. We witness individuals through personal effort and determination, along with group support, seeking guidance in practical daily living. They find solutions through specific application of the basic virtues to the character problems of life.

Growth means change — a ceaseless process of becoming different today from what one was yesterday, and different tomorrow from what one is today. Change comes from strength, and strength comes from God. God has the strength. It is ours for the asking.

May all who seek this strength through the program of Emotions Anonymous find even greater gifts — the power to love, to be at peace, to find meaning in life, and to be truly joyful. God will change me — if I will let Him.

Rev. Mark F. Mindrup, O.F.M.
Conv. Franciscan Retreats
Prior Lake, Minnesota (1978)

*   *   *   *   *

From a priest and spiritual director of Calix International:

When I first became a member of the fellowship of Alcoholics Anonymous, I was concerned with only one goal, and that was, of course, to obtain help in my struggle with the illness of alcoholism. I thank God and Alcoholics Anonymous daily that I have since enjoyed many years of happy sobriety.

However, as I grew in my understanding of the twelve-step program by living it, I became aware of subtle changes taking place in myself which I can describe only as attitudinal. My attitudes began to change drastically. As I tried to analyze what was taking place and why,

I became aware of the true significance of the Twelve Steps, not as stages to sobriety, but rather as directives to living. They became a way of life — guidelines to a good life, a full life, a wholesome life, a well balanced life, a mature life, a healthy life, and, therefore, a happy life. I began to see sobriety not as a goal but rather a bonus that was a logical consequence of the new attitudes which the living of the steps developed. I began to notice that I was constantly using the steps as the basis of my counseling sessions with people of a variety of difficulties.

As a priest I had often been called upon to act as a Father, Counselor and Confessor. I still daily ask God's pardon for my lack of insights. If I had ever helped anyone prior to my A.A. affiliation, I am certain it was only as an instrument of Divine Wisdom and not because of any human qualifications. I still feel very strongly today that our greatest responsibility and our greatest dignity is that God does use even the least of us as instruments of His love and healing power. However, He does expect us to develop, to sharpen, and to use the tools with which He has endowed us. For me, the tools are offered to us in the very practical, concise, and precise Twelve Steps to healthy living.

Somewhere along the line of my own growth in sanity I became aware of this way of life as an answer to practically all human ailments of an emotional nature. I had, at times, toyed with the idea of adapting the Twelve Steps of recovery to other human problems, particularly of an emotional nature. In my stupidity I envisioned a number of changes as being necessary. Imagine then my surprise and sheer joy when I finally heard of Emotions Anonymous. And marvel of marvels, it was adopted with the change of only one word. This gave me a little food for additional self-inventory, for I saw myself as still playing God and trying to improve His work. I truly believe that the twelve-step program is a twentieth century revelation of the Holy Spirit to counteract the emotional problems which our present pace of living is producing in almost plague-like proportions.

Since I became acquainted with EA, I have had numerous contacts with its members, both in helping to interpret and adapt the steps to life and as a fifth step person. I have seen some beautiful, even miraculous successes. This has proven EA will work. But, as in A.A., it will be successful only in the measure in which it is lived. Take nothing for granted, follow the steps religiously, be painfully honest with yourself, your God, and with others, and you too will begin to experience something beautiful happening to you. The program doesn't promise a life free from pain or problems, but it does promise a life of peace, serenity, and happiness in spite of the pains of normal human living.

Reverend Arnold Luger
Spiritual Director of Calix International
Minneapolis, Minnesota (1978)

* * * * *

From a minister and director of rehabilitation programs:

Emotions Anonymous has helped many people who are in need of this disciplined program for living and the fellowship which supports the program. The goal of EA has been to help people live as comfortably as possible inside their own skin. There isn't a single human being alive who could not prosper emotionally from EA, and it is with great respect and admiration that I endorse this program and refer many people to it.

Reverend Philip L. Hansen
Executive Director
Abbott-Northwestern Hospitals
Rehabilitation Programs
Minneapolis, Minnesota (1978)

* * * * *

BUSINESS PROFESSIONALS
From a lawyer:

The daily requirements of life with its extreme pressure upon each individual has often resulted in a breakdown of the fiber of happiness, stability, and self-esteem.

It has been my observation that an understanding and practice of the principles of Emotions Anonymous, as set forth in this book, has in many cases provided a vehicle by which the individual can accept, adjust, and function fully, adequately, and comfortably in our modern society.

Stanley J. Mosio
Attorney At Law
St. Paul, Minnesota (1978)

* * * * *

From a businessman:

When asked to serve as a trustee with Emotions Anonymous, I was honored and pleased to use my professional experience and skills in a useful service. Working with men and women who use the Twelve Steps of Emotions Anonymous to deal with their emotional lives is a humbling experience. The honesty and integrity of these people offer hope and inspiration for all.

It is an honor and privilege to recommend this book and its program to those looking for hope, faith, strength, or comfort. You will find them in the pages of this book. You will find them in the groups who use this book as a guide. And, of course, you will eventually find them in yourself, as many others have through practicing this program.

This book is a product of those who have found themselves or are finding themselves. It is the production of an organization, Emotions Anonymous, of these hardy souls whose stories fill its pages. This effort is their expression of gratitude and builds on the experience of those who came before them.

If you choose to participate, you will soon find you are joining a process of discovery — of yourself, of others, and of the universe. Use it well.

Robert C. Mead, President
RCM Enterprises, Inc.
Wayzata, Minnesota (1995)

How It Works

One day at a time

No one who has diligently followed our path has ever been known to fail. "Those who do not recover are people who cannot or will not completely give themselves to this simple program." * If you are hurting and want to change, you can. Recovery depends on being completely honest, open to new ideas, and willing to take the necessary actions.

These are the Twelve Steps which we follow in our program of recovery:

1. We admitted we were powerless over our emotions — that our lives had become unmanageable.

2. Came to believe that a Power greater than ourselves could restore us to sanity.

3. Made a decision to turn our will and our lives over to the care of God *as we understood Him.*

4. Made a searching and fearless moral inventory of ourselves.

5. Admitted to God, to ourselves, and to another human being the exact nature of our wrongs.

---

* *Alcoholics Anonymous* (New York: Alcoholics Anonymous World Services, Inc., 1976), p. 58.

6. Were entirely ready to have God remove all these defects of character.

7. Humbly asked Him to remove our shortcomings.

8. Made a list of all persons we had harmed and became willing to make amends to them all.

9. Made direct amends to such people wherever possible, except when to do so would injure them or others.

10. Continued to take personal inventory and when we were wrong promptly admitted it.

11. Sought through prayer and meditation to improve our conscious contact with God *as we understood Him,* praying only for knowledge of His will for us and the power to carry that out.

12. Having had a spiritual awakening as the result of these steps, we tried to carry this message and to practice these principles in all our affairs.

(*Permission to use the Twelve Steps of Alcoholics Anonymous for adaptation granted by A.A. World Services, Inc.*)

From the very beginning, we urge you to be fearless and thorough in following these steps. While some of them may seem too difficult, others unnecessary, and some even incomprehensible, you have everything to gain by trying them. Some of us tried to hold on to our old ways of thinking and behaving, but we found we could not grow in the program until we let go entirely and began to work these steps.

We discovered through this program a power greater than ourselves that helped us comprehend and begin working these steps in our daily lives. We learned we did not have to understand or work the program perfectly; we only had to do our best. By daily practice of these steps, we grew emotionally and spiritually. We discovered our true selves. We found recovery. You can too.

Step One

We admitted we were powerless over our emotions –
that our lives had become unmanageable.

Powerless

When we first came to Emotions Anonymous and heard people say they were powerless, many of us rebelled; certainly we were not powerless. We may have refused to say powerless because we disliked the idea of powerlessness so much. We may have felt frightened or threatened by this idea.

Perhaps you too are uncertain as to whether you are really powerless over your emotions. Look at some of these descriptions of how powerlessness affected many of us and see if any apply to you.

- We were unable to start or stop an emotion.
- We felt helpless and, perhaps, hopeless.
- We could not get well by ourselves no matter how hard we tried.
- We tried analyzing, but it did not work.
- We were not able to change by using just our willpower.
- We were not self-sufficient no matter how much we wanted to be; we needed other people.
- We were powerless over our feelings, positive and negative.

Do you ever become angry with someone and try to make that anger go away by using logic and reason? Do you ever feel guilty about something and try to rationalize it away? Do you ever feel lonely even with many people in your life? Have you ever felt afraid when reason said there was nothing to fear? Do you ever say or think, "Why does everything have to happen to me?" If so, you are, we believe, powerless over your emotions.

Our acceptance of powerlessness does not mean we are bad or lack responsibility in other areas of our lives. It means our emotions are causing our behaviors to be other than what we would like. When we come to realize we are powerless, we can then look for a new direction and begin to change. We can see our limitations and acknowledge the reality of our lives.

UNMANAGEABLE

Are our lives truly unmanageable? We ask ourselves if any of these statements apply to us.

- The more we try to control our behavior, the more out of control we become.
- We think the people around us make life unmanageable, but the more we try to change others the more unmanageable our lives become. We are powerless over other people and cannot change them.
- We are oversensitive and touchy about what others say. In our self-centeredness we take the everyday occurrences and actions of other people too personally and too seriously.
- We do not talk to others because we are sure they would not want to talk to us.
- We are unable to accomplish ordinary tasks.
- We have so many problems in our lives we do not know where to begin.
- We feel different and alone.

Our lives become unmanageable for a variety of reasons. Loneliness, shame, insecurity, shyness, or low self-esteem are often among them. Other factors may include fear of rejection, fear of failure, fear of not belonging, fear of being different, feelings of inadequacy, rejection of self, self-centeredness, self-denial, or fear of involvement. We may be experiencing life through a haze of hostility and resentment because of past traumas.

Many symptoms can indicate that our lives are unmanageable. Often physical and psychosomatic illnesses are symptoms. These can include ulcers; stomach pains; headaches; hypertension; skin disorders; heart and circulatory irregularities; urinary and intestinal disorders; or back, muscle, and joint complaints. Of course, all physical symptoms should be evaluated medically, but if no medical reason is found, we must suspect an emotional basis and start looking for the cause.

Compulsive perfectionism can be another symptom. If we cannot do something perfectly, we consider ourselves failures. We may react by becoming passive; we sit back and accept whatever others do or say. We may not be happy doing this and probably begin to storm on the inside, but we are not capable of or we fear asserting ourselves in various situations. This can lead to aggression in areas where we feel more in control. For example, if we have difficulty with co-workers or employers, we may come home and take out our frustrations on family members. Another way of reacting to our perfectionism is by rejecting whatever others do. Nothing anyone else does or says is acceptable to us. We criticize everything and, as a result, our relationships with those around us become filled with emotional upheaval.

We may be nervous and panicky or suffer from depression or anxiety. We may be accident prone. We may fantasize about how wonderful life will be when things change. We probably worry a great deal, have trouble sleeping, withdraw from others, become irritable and perhaps even abuse those we love. We may even feel others are talking about us, watching our every move or are out to get us. Abnormal rage and temper tantrums are often symptoms that make us realize something is very wrong. We may be destructive, violent, or even homicidal. We may feel suicidal and may even attempt suicide. For many in EA, these extremes of emotion made us realize that our lives were unmanageable.

Some of us do not have clear-cut psychological problems, but we are living in a way that does not produce much happiness. We are often apathetic. We procrastinate and act phony. We often are judgmental and criticize others because it seems to make us feel better about ourselves, yet we may also let others walk all over us. We seldom say no to requests and often take on too much. We may be filled with feelings of self-pity, resentment, anger, jealousy, envy, greed, intolerance, impatience, selfishness, or any of the many other feelings which are characteristic of unmanageable lives.

Some of us try to rationalize our feelings away. We also may try various ways to escape from our feelings. Some escapes are pills, alcohol, food, unhealthy sexual activity, gambling, shopping, or work. We may focus on needing to rescue others from their problems. Even talking, silence, sleep, reading, exercise, travel, or going to school may become an escape when used to excess. We may be a television or movie addict who lets the rest of the world go by. Anything used to excess can interfere with having a balanced life and prevent us from facing and dealing with our pain.

When our particular escape does not work, we look elsewhere for the help we so desperately need. In turning to EA and the Twelve Steps as a possible answer, we are admitting we have hit our emotional bottom. This is different for each person. For some it means life is uncomfortable and we are looking for a way to be happy. Some of us reach the depths of despair and may need treatment by a mental health professional, medication, or hospitalization. Still others come to Emotions Anonymous in an effort to help another person, but once there, realize we also need help. One thing we all have in common is that this emotional bottom is where we decide we want to do something today to change our life. We are sick and tired of our old ways; we are tired of being the way we are. We realize our life will remain unmanageable if we do not change.

ADMITTING

Admitting we cannot manage our lives is not easy. It is not easy to admit our self-centeredness, self-pity, and resentments. It is difficult to stop blaming others for the way we are and the way we behave. We say, "If my spouse were different," or "If it weren't for my children, my parents, my in-laws, my boss, my job, my neighbors, my house, my car, the climate — anything or anybody — I wouldn't be like this."

Through Step One we begin to learn to accept our emotions as they are and not allow them to control our behavior. As we learn to accept our emotions, we are better able to manage our lives. We can make conscious choices in response to our emotions rather than just reacting and having our emotions manage us. We begin to take responsibility for our lives, regardless of who or what may have influenced us in the past.

This first step is one of honesty and humility. Admitting our human limitations frees us from hiding our imperfections from ourselves and others, thus allowing us to face the reality of our situation. At first, Step One may seem a step of despair, but we learn there is hope. We find we are not alone; there is help. In Step Two we find the strength to restore our health as we begin to rely on spiritual guidance, and our hope grows.

STEP TWO

*Came to believe that a Power greater than ourselves
could restore us to sanity.*

This is a step of hope. Since we do not have the power to make ourselves well, we need to develop a belief, and then faith, in a power which is greater than ourselves – a Higher Power.

POWER GREATER THAN OURSELVES

When we came to EA, some of us had no concept of a Higher Power. Others were very confused about the nature of God. Some viewed God only as something to be feared or someone capable of punishment. Others believed they had a good relationship with their Higher Power, yet were baffled that this did not seem to solve their emotional problems. Some were searching for something in which to believe. Still others had decided there was no God.

In Step Two it is our responsibility to formulate our own belief system. We need not follow anyone else's path. Those who have a religious faith which is comfortable to them use that belief. Those who are unclear about what to believe in need only to start exploring the possibilities. This step will work for each of us long before we have a complete idea of our belief system.

Developing this powerful relationship is not always easy and requires us to look honestly at our feelings and beliefs about spiritual matters. It does not matter how this greater power is defined; we simply must develop a working concept of a Higher Power. It does not matter in what or whom we believe. What matters is that we do believe there is something or someone with greater power than we have and will use that power to help us recover. This can be any idea of God, the EA group (the power of many people working together for recovery is greater than one person's power), nature (a force certainly greater than we are), the idea of universal principles, or anything we can accept as being greater than our individual selves.

No longer able to manage our lives, to live at peace with ourselves and others, we are forced to turn to a Higher Power out of desperation. Everything — our growth in EA, serenity, happiness, and well-being — depends upon faith in a power greater than our own limited resources. Faith is belief in and reliance on a power greater than ourselves. We do not have to make drastic changes to be eligible for our Higher Power's help. This power is available to us right where we are. If we have difficulty developing this relationship, we can begin by trusting another human being, perhaps a sponsor or someone else from our EA group. Step Two requires us to admit the existence of a power greater than ourselves. Once we realize we are not all powerful, we can stop trying to be God and let God be God.

Many of us find through working the Twelve Steps that our concept of a Higher Power develops into a deep personal relationship with a spiritual being, a relationship not possible before the program. A paradox of the program is that being powerless, we find a power to help us.

CAME TO BELIEVE

First we came to a meeting where we saw others in recovery. We began to believe that help was available. Some of us became aware of our poor self-worth. We did not feel worthy of help, whether from the group or from a Higher Power. Then we came to realize we were all equal and as important and valuable as everyone else. Yes, we too were worthy of help. At first, we were very skeptical about this step, but knowing we had little to lose, we took the risk to believe. In time, we came to believe a Higher Power could restore us to sanity, given willingness and open-mindedness on our part.

As we examined our spiritual lives, many of us saw how we were defying God, perhaps because God had not delivered what we had prayed for in the past. Perhaps we had met with some great sorrow or disappointment and thought God had deserted us. We may have experienced illness and asked God to make us well, but nothing seemed to happen. Some of us had been abused by our parents or other authority figures, and we have great difficulty with the idea of God as a loving parent. We may be defiant about spiritual matters because we are afraid to give up our control.

In EA we found a Higher Power who was helpful and supportive. We learned to let go of old beliefs which were destructive to us and to seek our own understanding of spiritual matters. We discovered that by attending meetings and working the program we could recognize and accept new principles discarding those which were false or harmful to us.

Some of us thought we were full of faith when we came into the program. We prayed, attended church regularly, and did what we thought were the right things to do. We were convinced that since we tried to be good members of our particular religion, our lives should not be so troubled. We found that quality must be sought in regard to faith, not quantity. We learned belief does not automatically turn into faith. We can believe in God, yet not trust that God will help us. We recognized our own practice of faith needed to be more vital. We opened our minds to a new and more relevant relationship to our Higher Power.

Others of us looked with envy at those who believed. Weren't they lucky? Perhaps by coming to the meetings we would come to believe also. But we learn that believing does not just happen; we must work at it. We need to be willing to invest time and open-minded investigation into developing a concept of a Higher Power that will work for us. With belief comes faith and a willingness to trust in something previously unknown, to trust in a Higher Power to restore us to that sanity we so desperately want.

Believing in a power greater than ourselves is different from having faith in a Higher Power. We do not simply wish for more faith. To develop our faith we must use it. We show little faith if we continue to hold onto our fears and anxieties. When we recognize these are making our lives unmanageable and that we are powerless, we turn them over to our Higher Power. We believe our Higher Power will take care of us. Faith comes as we see the miracles our Higher Power works in our lives and in the lives of others. Miracles are not just big, grand events. We gain faith as we look at what is going on around us and begin to see each gift or simple intervention which is a miracle produced by our Higher Power. As we begin to recognize these and give the credit to our Higher Power, our understanding, belief, and faith grows. Our lives may improve without believing in a Higher Power, but we cannot reach the ultimate serenity without true belief in a power greater than ourselves.

RESTORE US TO SANITY

Restore means we will be brought back to health and strength. How wonderful! Some of us remember having had emotional well-being. Some cannot recall a time when we did not feel at odds with life. We find comfort in the idea that at some time in the past we had been healthy and can be so once again. Our lost sense of well-being can be restored to us. This is the sense of hope provided by Step Two.

The word sanity in Step Two is difficult to accept for some of us. Sanity is sane thinking, common sense. The dictionary defines sanity as reasonable behavior. We need only look at our past behavior — temper tantrums, uncontrolled anger, compulsive behaviors, silence, excessive sleep, or excessive anything — to know our behavior was certainly not sane or rational. We hear others refer to insanity not as dementia or outright craziness, but as repeating the same actions or behaviors over and over again and expecting different results. After giving the matter some thought we had to admit the word sanity is appropriate.

The more fully we admit we need to be restored to sanity, the more we will seek help from our Higher Power as a solution to our problems and difficulties. The more fully we believe our Higher Power can restore us to sanity, the more we will seek that help, and the more willing we will be to make our third-step decision, to turn our will and lives over to our Higher Power.

STEP THREE
Made a decision to turn our will and our lives over to the care of God as we understood Him.

In Step Three we are asked to demonstrate our faith. We no longer merely accept the idea of a Higher Power which can help us, but we allow this spiritual power to direct our lives. We stop fighting and resisting. We let go and let God.

Now we have an opportunity to build a new life. We have faced our dilemma and know the more we deny or fight our feelings, the more the depression, anxieties, and fears close in. We had to stop trying to be self-sufficient if we want to get well. Looking at our lives we realized on our own we had not done such a great job. Since emotions are not tangible things, we must admit we cannot change ourselves by willpower alone.

The first three steps are pivotal. The acceptance of ourselves, of others, and of our situations is the basis of these three steps. It is through them that we set the foundation for working the rest of the program. Therefore, we come back to them time and time again.

Acceptance is not apathy. Acceptance is: "This is who I am; this is the best I can do today. Stop fighting." However, acceptance does not mean we resign ourselves to an unkind fate. It simply means we can live today without fighting things which we cannot change. Apathy says, "I give up. It isn't worth it. I don't care; I don't want to try." Apathy demonstrates how little regard we have for ourselves. It is giving in to the distorted view that there is no hope for us. Acceptance frees us to change. Apathy keeps us locked into our emotional and spiritual illness.

We can begin to practice this step at times of indecision or emotional distress by saying the Serenity Prayer:

"God grant me the serenity to accept the things I cannot change, courage to change the things I can, and wisdom to know the difference."

MADE A DECISION

In spite of all the hope we feel for our possible recovery, many find this third-step decision difficult. Some of us want iron-clad guarantees before we decide to turn things over to our Higher Power. Others are fearful of making such a commitment. We are not even sure we can live up to this commitment. What if we make this decision and things do not turn out the way we want? After being in the program awhile, we realize that if we want to progress we have to make this decision. We see how the lives of others improve as they take this step. We can choose to take it also.

When we first make the decision to turn our lives over to a Higher Power, we feel good about it. We may perhaps be uneasy or frightened that we will not be acceptable to our Higher Power. We soon learn, however, that when we surrender ourselves totally just as we are — symptoms, feelings, imperfections — the way opens for our Higher Power to supply us with what we need.

TURN OVER OUR WILL AND OUR LIVES

We find we cannot live by self-will alone; many of us have tried and failed. Willpower is never as successful as we hope. After all, other people have willpower too, and we often find ourselves in conflict with them when we pit our will against theirs. In our efforts to control situations we may show generosity, self-sacrifice, consideration, or kindness, but more often we are driven by fears, resentments, self-pity, or self-delusion and we end up stepping on the toes of others. They may retaliate and hurt us. We find our words and actions have often placed us in a position which allows us to be hurt. We have to admit that basically our troubles in such instances are of our own making. They arise out of our misdirected self-will though we often have not recognized this. In fact, in reacting blindly to our emotions, our self-will has run rampant, causing us to behave poorly. It is essential that we rid ourselves of this self-centeredness, but we are unable to do so by wishing it away or using our own willpower. We have to have the help of our Higher Power.

Before we can turn our will over to a Higher Power, we have to give up the idea that we must be entirely self-sufficient. Making this decision demonstrates a commitment to use the program. We are willing to try something new. However, we cannot just fold our hands and say, "God, do everything." As God supplies the power, we are the ones who have to take the actions and make the changes needed to achieve a healthier life.

It does no good to analyze God's will. We do not always know what is God's will for us, nor does it even matter if we do. As we develop a partnership with our Higher Power and begin to know ourselves, we begin to recognize the direction that seems spiritually right for us.

The key to working this step is our willingness to turn over our will and our lives to the care of the God of our understanding. We may be reluctant to do this until we have some level of trust that our Higher Power will actually take care of us. Developing caring, trusting relationships with other people paves the way for many of us to trust our Higher Power. At first, we may decide to relinquish only those parts of our lives which are causing us the most pain. From this beginning we can build our confidence as we see positive changes take place in our lives.

God as We Understood Him

For those of us who have negative feelings about religion and God, this step is a potential stumbling block. We can accept many of the ideas of Step Two, but some of us feel this specific definition of a Higher Power is going too far. If we are offended by, or unable to use, the words "God" or "Him," we can choose other words that work better for us in describing our Higher Power. We need to remember we are all free to define our Higher Power in any way we wish.

Many of us have believed since childhood in a God of fear and punishment. We think that for God to accept us we must be obedient and strive for perfection. Since God is watching us and keeping track of our wrongdoings, we will surely never measure up when the final tally is taken. We feel we are doomed. With this concept of God, it can be very difficult to look at this step and think about turning our will and our lives over to God. We need an image of a caring Higher Power who can restore us to sanity and give us the strength to change. If we do not have a concept of a loving God, we ask our Higher Power to help us develop one. We become willing to examine our spiritual beliefs and learn to trust a power greater than ourselves.

The Care of God

When we let go, many remarkable things follow. Being caring and all powerful, God provides what we need as we let go. We find courage where we had none before. As we become more secure in this powerful relationship, we lose our self-centeredness and become less focused on petty matters. We are freed from the agony of trying to be God ourselves. We release to God the responsibility of managing our lives and the lives of those around us. We feel less resentful and defensive. We become interested in contributing to life around us. As we experience this new power in our lives, we begin to enjoy peace of mind. As we discover we can more easily face life, we become more conscious of our Higher Power working in our lives. We begin to lose our fear of the past, the present, and the future. We begin to live one day at a time.

We can now put ourselves in God's care by making this humble request:

> "God, I offer myself to you, to build and to do with
> me as you wish. Help me let go of my self-centeredness,
> so I can better recognize your will for me. Help me
> overcome my difficulties so others can see how your love,
> wisdom, and strength allows me to change. Thank you
> for being with me. May I do your will always."*

We found a loving God. At last we can abandon ourselves entirely to the care of our Higher Power. Now we are ready for the vigorous action of Step Four.

STEP FOUR
Made a searching and fearless moral inventory of ourselves.

Our faith in a Higher Power, along with our decision to allow this Power to guide us, provides the courage we need to do a personal inventory. This inventory is an honest look at ourselves, perhaps for the first time. It is a very necessary look. We try to be as objective as possible because we need this information for our recovery.

We may want clear-cut directions on how to do the inventory, however, there are many ways to proceed. We find talking to others who have done theirs or reviewing the many guides which are available can help us gather ideas. Each person does a personal inventory in the way that seems best to him or her. However, we do not let perfectionism get in the way of this step. There is no perfect way to do our inventory. Sometimes we add more of this inventory later since our self-honesty increases as we recover. The important thing is to begin.

A thorough and healthy inventory usually includes a balance of assets and defects. In doing our personal inventory we write down both positive and negative character traits. It is necessary to get a true picture of ourselves, so we seek out our strengths as well as our weaknesses.

---

*Adapted from *Alcoholics Anonymous* (New York: Alcoholics Anonymous World Services, Inc., 1976), p. 63.

It is important to write down this inventory in order to achieve an honest appraisal. It is less likely for us to rationalize or forget what is written down, and, therefore, we can deal with the issues more objectively.

SEARCHING

We search honestly and thoroughly covering all aspects of our lives. We list experiences and behaviors from the past which bother us. We do not knowingly exclude anything. While it sometimes appears that the feelings we list are defects of character, they are not. Feelings are neither good nor bad. We discover that the way we have reacted to our emotions has shaped our character and the manner in which we conduct ourselves in the world. We need to look honestly at the beliefs and attitudes on which our character is based. We search out the reasons which cause us to feel we have failed.

Self-honesty brings self-acceptance and a realistic understanding of where and how we can change. We have no defects which are unique; we are all human. Anything we allow ourselves to become aware of can be changed. It is necessary for us to look within.

FEARLESS

Fearlessness is the attitude we need to go ahead and take our inventory. To be fearless means accepting the challenge to be open and honest in looking within, regardless of our reluctance or apprehensions. Our Higher Power gives us the courage to do this. As we proceed with our inventory, uncomfortable and uneasy feelings sometimes arise. Looking at ourselves and past behaviors can cause buried feelings to surface. It helps to remember that our source of support and guidance in completing this inventory is our Higher Power. We may need to stop for awhile, talk to someone, or go back to Step Three.

The more unrealistic self-image we have, the more difficult it is to uncover our defects. There is pain in every healing process and the only way out of our pain is to move through it. As we grow and face our pain in Step Four, the way is opened to the serenity we seek.

MORAL INVENTORY

Morality is our sense of right and wrong, and it is an outward reflection of our inner self. Our prejudices, intolerance, criticisms, fears, and guilt are all a part of our morality, as are selfishness, egotism, and resentment. Morality comes from beliefs and attitudes which, starting in childhood, we accepted as truths. Some of these beliefs may be erroneous. Our attitudes may be unrealistic or based on conditions that no longer exist in our lives. We may be living according to someone else's morality rather than our own. As we discover what we truly believe, we are able to act more in accordance with those beliefs. The purpose of this inventory is to uncover the ineffective behaviors we have developed and to look at the ways we have been controlled by them.

Among the important things we deal with in our inventory are resentments. These feelings of ill-will toward other people or institutions destroy peace of mind. When we resent someone or something, we unknowingly allow that person or thing to control us. It hurts us, though it may not hurt the person we resent. They probably are not even aware of it. Harboring deep resentments leads only to a life of frustration and unhappiness. Because of this, we list in our inventory resentments we have had toward people, institutions, or principles. We ask ourselves why we are still angry toward them. We then describe how these resentments have affected the way we think, feel, or behave. Is it our pride, self-esteem, ambition, personal relationships, or financial security that is hurt or threatened? If we can identify the emotion which results, we write this down.

The following are examples we might list.

- *I resent* my boss *because* he never gives positive feedback, is critical, promoted someone else instead of me. *This affects my* financial security, self-esteem, pride, relationships with co-workers. *I feel* I am a failure at my job; fear of failure.

- *I resent* my parents *because* they treat me like a child, don't respect my abilities, complain that I never write or call. *This affects my* pride, family relations, self-esteem, affection toward

55

them. *I feel* I am not acceptable as I am, that I must be who they want me to be; fear of rejection.

- *I resent* my car *because* it is a lemon, always breaking down. I can't afford a new one. *This affects my* pride, sense of security, independence. *I feel* I was stupid to buy it, that I seem foolish to others; fear of making decisions.

Looking at the above examples, we see the word *fear* in every one. In many situations fear is the first emotion to take over. Fear is the result of threats to our self-esteem, pride, and well-being. When we look at our resentments, we find they are usually a reaction to being afraid. We do not like to be afraid so we cover it up with resentments which give us a false sense of being in control.

In our inventory we list our fears. We review our past conduct to see how these fears have influenced our thinking, controlled our behavior, and affected relationships with others. Had fear caused us to be selfish, dishonest, or inconsiderate? Whom have we hurt? Do we feel guilty? Do we unjustifiably feel jealousy, suspicion, or bitterness? We write all this down.

As we grew up we may have acquired guilt, shame, or embarrassment for our sexual thoughts, feelings, and experiences. Doing our inventory helps us bring these tormenting ghosts out into the open and be honest about our sexual experiences. We had to stop judging others or ourselves. Hiding this guilt and shame only keeps us from becoming well. We will continue to reject ourselves and others until we accept our human limitations.

Continuing our inventory, we list all other aspects of ourselves at which we need to look. If we hold deep secrets, we write them down. Anything, when acknowledged, can be worked through without it becoming a continual attitude or behavior problem. These negative attitudes or behaviors are defects of character and are the driving force behind the wrongs we have done. For example, to deny our feeling of self-pity encourages our attitude of "Poor me, I've got it so tough." Understanding this, we realize we are human and not bad because we feel this way. We can accept that this characteristic is part of us for the present. A defect of character will become less of a problem as we are willing to work on it in Steps Five, Six, and Seven.

OF OURSELVES

While writing our inventory we concentrate only on ourselves. This is our inventory, not another person's. We consider only our own involvement in situations even when something may have not been entirely our fault. In doing so we become aware of how self-centered we are and how our ego keeps us in this self-centeredness. We see where we have contributed to our own difficulties by being selfish, dishonest, self-seeking, and frightened.

If we are thorough about our personal inventory, we write down a lot. We deal with our resentments and fears and begin to see their terrible destructiveness. As we list things on paper, we are better able to see our faults and admit our wrongs. We list people we have hurt by our behavior and use this list later in our eighth step. We begin to learn tolerance and patience toward ourselves and others.

Through this honest personal inventory, we become more aware of our humanness. We begin to see the character defects that make us uncomfortable, that cause us difficulty with ourselves and others. We also look for our assets because our goal is to build a healthy, realistic image of who we are. We list our good qualities, in spite of how difficult it may be at first to admit them, and are surprised how many there are.

With this tangible evidence of our willingness to look at ourselves honestly, we are ready to move forward to Step Five.

STEP FIVE

Admitted to God, to ourselves, and to another human being
the exact nature of our wrongs.

All of EA's Twelve Steps ask us to go against our normal inclinations. They all deflate our egos, and this step is perhaps the greatest ego deflator of them all. Here we are asked to admit exactly what we have done wrong, not just to ourselves and God, but to someone else as well. It was not enough to write things down in our fourth-step inventory. We need to talk about these things — out loud and in person. As unsettling as this may sound to us, this process will prove to be of great benefit in our recovery. Step Five is absolutely necessary in producing an enduring serenity and peace of mind. Thinking about this step will do us no good; we gather our courage once again and go into action.

Admitting

We already admitted our wrongs by writing our inventory, but solitary self-appraisal is not enough. For instance, too much guilt can cause us to exaggerate our shortcomings and anxiety or pride can cause us to minimize our defects. Sometimes our self-centeredness keeps us thinking other people are at fault for our behavior, or we are under constant fear and tension which makes us want to escape from reality. Admitting who we really are to another person is the only way to get a true picture of ourselves.

If we were honest in writing our inventory, we may have included certain distressing and humiliating memories which we hoped would remain our secret. We are certain no one would ever understand or accept us if they knew what we had done or what had happened to us, so we worry about sharing our inventory as this step asks us to do. We may feel lonely or isolated which is further reason why we need to admit these things to another person.

Admitting the truth about ourselves permits us to enter into new relationships with ourselves and with our world. Admitting means acknowledging those areas which we need to change.

Exact Nature of Our Wrongs

It is necessary to share the specific examples we wrote down in Step Four, not simply to say we feel resentful, fearful, and guilty. We have to deal with the exact nature of our wrongs by revealing them to someone else. The easiest and surest way to be specific is to read aloud to another person what we have written. This way, we are certain to leave nothing out.

When doing our fifth step, we go over everything in our inventory. It is necessary to share all of our inventory, for if we knowingly omit something, that will likely prolong our misery. If we are determined to get well, we will be honest. By holding back nothing, we are on the road to recovery.

To God, to Ourselves, and to Another Human Being

It is important to admit our inventory to God, to ourselves, and to another person. If we leave out one of these three, our fifth step will not provide the strong foundation we need for the rest of the program. Just as a chair or table cannot stand with one of its legs missing, so our recovery will not be steady unless we have revealed our inventory to another person, to our Higher Power, and to ourselves.

We developed a partnership with our Higher Power in Steps Two and Three, so it seems less embarrassing to share our secrets and negative character traits with our Higher Power than facing another person. After all, God knows everything we have done, yet still loves and accepts us. When actually doing the fifth step, many chose to begin with a prayer, perhaps the Serenity Prayer, as a way of inviting our Higher Power to be a part of this step.

It is in the telling to someone else and, consequently, listening to ourselves that we begin to get a true understanding of who we actually are. Here we no longer try to maintain that public image which often does not fit with our private selves. By being honest with another person we confirm that we are being honest with ourselves and with God.

The fifth step is best taken with a person who has a working knowledge of the twelve-step program because it is very important that this person understand what we are trying to accomplish. We do not want him or her to excuse our behavior or try to fix us, but simply to be the witness to our honest inventory. Our fifth-step person may be a member of a twelve-step program or a counselor, clergy, doctor, or similar professional person. While this person may give insight, encouragement, or suggestions, he or she is primarily a listener. For this to be a positive and successful experience, it is important that this person be trustworthy and understanding, someone who will not betray our confidence and with whom we feel comfortable. This person must also be accepting and non-judgmental.

We gain a great deal by completing Step Five. We will usually rid ourselves of our sense of isolation and loneliness. We gain the feeling of belonging, a sense of kinship with other people, and a closeness to our Higher Power. Some of us experience an immediate feeling of relief as our fear and pain subsides, and a healing tranquility comes over us. Others feel vibrant and alive, as if "walking on cloud nine." Because we were led to an understanding, accepting fifth-step person, we realize God really does love us. Many who take this step actually feel the presence of a personal Higher Power for the first time. Even those who already have faith become conscious of God as never before.

With others the relief comes more gradually, and there is not a sudden feeling of release. Generally over the next several days, we become aware that things are not bothering us as much and we feel better about ourselves. The terrible burden of shame is lifted and a pervading sense of peace takes over.

As we experience support and compassion from the person to whom we share our inventory, we feel forgiven. At the same time, honestly sharing what we have discovered about ourselves helps us to forgive ourselves and others.

Immediately following the fifth step, many of us find a quiet place to review carefully what has transpired. We thank our Higher Power for the strength and courage given to us. We feel gratitude for the new level of trust our relationship with the God of our understanding has attained.

Now that we have gained much self-awareness and have shared this awareness, we are ready for the remaining steps of the program.

STEP SIX

Were entirely ready to have God remove all these defects of character.

By doing our inventory in Step Four and sharing it in Step Five, we learned a great deal about ourselves. Behind our resentments, fears, and wrongs we discovered some defects of character. These defects of character are our negative habits of thinking and acting, our automatic reactions to life, our ineffective behaviors. Now, in Step Six we strive to further identify these defects of character and become willing to have them removed.

WERE ENTIRELY READY

This sounds so simple, for wouldn't anyone be ready to get rid of characteristics which cause life to be unmanageable? Of course we are ready! However, the nature of our illness is such that readiness is not as easy to acquire as we might hope. We expect it to be easy to change now that we really understand ourselves, but often we are surprised to find how difficult it actually is to change our thought patterns, attitudes, and behaviors. We are so comfortable with some of our defects that we do not even want to think about getting rid of them. They have been a part of our lives for such a long time that we depend on them. We depend on some defects for our sense of identity or to maintain the illusion that we are in control of our lives. Occasionally we rationalize that some of them are insignificant and not really causing much difficulty. However, Step Six is very clear: that we must be ready for all defects to be removed. We cannot cling to any of them and think we will never give them up. In order to make further progress in our spiritual and emotional growth, we have to become ready to let go of all ineffective behaviors and let God help us to change.

As we focus on Step Six, we become aware of how deeply ingrained most of our character defects are. The process of taking inventory revealed how many of our defects developed as defenses against harm or trauma we experienced in the past. Because of the deep roots of our defects, it is clear that at this stage we may not be able to face all of our defects at once. However, we have to strive for the objective of being entirely ready to have all defects removed, often by preparing to have a few defects removed at a time. To do this, we need patience and persistence, since this transformation of character is a lifelong process. We also have to accept the fact that we probably will never achieve perfection in practicing this step. Accepting this is the beginning of becoming ready to let go of one of our biggest character defects, the need to be perfect.

It sometimes seems that no matter how much willpower we exert, negative behaviors, attitudes, and thoughts continue to plague us. To move past them we have to move from just wanting to be willing to actually being willing to live differently. The key for us is willingness; until we are willing to make some attempt to be ready to have our defects removed, there is no way they would disappear by themselves. To do this, we pray for the willingness to have them removed.

Have God Remove All These Defects of Character

We make a beginning by picking out the defect which causes us the most pain. To reduce our dependence on it we deliberately replace it, as much as possible, with the opposite character asset. For example, if procrastination is a problem, we would try to do things in a timely manner. We act as if this character defect were already removed. By making conscious, healthy choices in our thoughts and actions we demonstrate to our Higher Power and to ourselves that we are, in fact, ready and willing for the defect to be removed. Here we have another opportunity to give up self-will. If we hold on to our character defects, we do our will; if we let go, we do God's will.

Most of us want to be well yesterday. However, we did not become emotionally sick overnight, and we cannot expect to get well in a short time. Because as human beings we are limited in the power we possess, we must go on to Step Seven and humbly ask the God of our understanding for help in removing our deeply rooted behaviors and attitudes.

STEP SEVEN
Humbly asked Him to remove our shortcomings.

In Step Six we became ready to have the God of our understanding remove our character defects. We did this by becoming acutely aware of our defects and developing the willingness to let go of them. We tried to bring our personal will into alignment with the will of our Higher Power. In Step Seven we continue this process by asking God to remove our shortcomings. Shortcomings are the actions caused by our character defects. These behaviors demonstrate where we have come up short of reaching our potential. We need to be rid of our defects in order to correct our behavior and to live happy, serene, and manageable lives. As defects are removed, assets replace them. All of this will be done by our Higher Power as we demonstrate our readiness and ask that it be done. The efforts are ours, but the results come from God.

HUMBLY ASKED HIM

Humility is the key to working Step Seven. When we first come into the program many of us misunderstand the meaning of humility. Some think humility means feeling inferior to other people. Others have been taught not to act too self-confident or to talk about the good in themselves because that appears conceited and, therefore, not humble. Some confuse humility with humiliation. Mistakenly we think we must be doormats for other people, that we must be meek and non-assertive. Our character defects cause us to feel hopeless, worthless, depressed, and anxious — in other words, humiliated, but this was not humility.

As we progress in the program we learn what humility is. The origin of the word humble is humus, meaning soil or ground. Humility is having our feet planted firmly on the ground, having good basic values and standing on them. It is having a clear view of reality, seeing the truth about ourselves. It is a realistic sense of one's position in relation to God and to other people. It involves knowing we are no better or worse than any other person. When we are humble, we do not compare ourselves to others because comparing only causes us to feel superior or inferior. This may cause us to focus on others and avoid looking at our own character defects.

To be humble is to be willing to learn to be open minded to a new way of life. Deciding to ask for help and using the twelve-step program to transform our lives are steps toward humility. Humility encompasses the qualities of honesty, acceptance, looking for the good, and trust.

Our work on the previous six steps has brought us some humility, and we have become aware of our dependency on the God of our understanding. We try to set aside our own willful desires and to seek out God's will in our lives. We have also become aware that we may have an unhealthy dependency on one or more people. We feel we cannot survive without them, that we need them in order to be whole or safe. Of course we need people, but not in unhealthy dependent ways. We realize a large part of our growth depends on sharing with others and building meaningful, interdependent relationships.

What can we gain by being humble? Humility helps us transform failure and misery into the assets of success and happiness. Humility allows us freely to share the details of our personal history to help others who are suffering with emotional problems.

Remove Our Shortcomings

We had to turn away from proud resistance and ask a power greater than ourselves to remove our shortcomings. When ready, we humbly ask,

> "Higher Power, I am now willing to totally give myself
> to you, the good and bad. I ask that you now remove
> from me every single defect of character which prevents
> me from being useful to you and to others. Grant me
> strength, as I go out to do your will." *

If we are entirely ready to have our shortcomings removed and

---

*Adapted from *Alcoholics Anonymous* (New York: Alcoholics Anonymous World Services, Inc., 1976), p. 76.

believe that our Higher Power will remove them, then character assets which we need will replace them. Changes occur though not always according to our time frame or exactly as we have planned. If something is not immediately removed, we realized that we need to be patient, and we probably have more work to do. Perhaps we are not yet entirely ready to let go of this particular defect. We may still need a defect because there is some lesson yet to be learned from it. We may have made demands instead of humbly asking God for help.

As we grow in humility, we acquire a new understanding of our relationship with God. Now, in Steps Eight and Nine, we work toward improving our relationships with other people.

STEP EIGHT
Made a list of all persons we had harmed
and became willing to make amends to them all.

The previous seven steps have been a process of changing our self-centered attitudes and actions by looking within ourselves. It is now time to repair damage done in the past by making the necessary amends. Step Eight helps us restore personal relationships and lifts us out of our isolation. With it we can accept responsibility for our past in order to let go of the old pain. Releasing the past brings healing and allows us to live in harmony with ourselves and others.

MADE A LIST OF PERSONS WE HAD HARMED
When we did Steps Four and Five we revealed some of the wrongs we had done to others. In Step Eight we examine our fourth-step inventory to see where we need to improve relations with the people in our lives. From our inventory we begin to list the people we have harmed. Looking back over our lives we see where we have been at fault. We review our lives as far back as we can remember, focusing on whom we have hurt and in what ways we have hurt them. We list them on paper to show that we are serious about completing this step. Our list

might include family members, relatives, friends, neighbors, public contacts, and business associates. We might also list places of employ- ment, stores, businesses, or other institutions where we have stolen something or caused damage.

Fear and pride often cause us to resist this step and hinder our making a complete list. If this is the case, we work on these character defects through Steps Six and Seven. We do the best we can for now, realizing that as our awareness and honesty grow we will be able to add other names to our list who have not occurred to us yet.

If our list includes almost everyone we know, we have to take another look at it. Some of us may indeed have been very domineering, aggressive, or sarcastic and, therefore, may have hurt many people. On the other hand, our self-centeredness and tendency to believe the world revolves around us sometimes causes us to include unnecessary names because we exaggerate the importance of our smallest word or deed. In reality, some people we list probably will not even know what we are talking about if we try to apologize. However, we do not use this as an excuse for leaving out a name. When in doubt we put down the names of all we think we have harmed and re-evaluate our list with the help of an objective person when the time comes to actually make amends.

Many of us realize the person hurt the most has been ourself, and we have to include our own name on this list. We may have hurt ourselves by blaming ourselves for things that were beyond our control or by judging ourselves too harshly. We must accept and forgive ourselves if we are to accept and forgive others.

BECAME WILLING

Many of us react with disbelief, anger, or fear when we first become aware that we might owe amends to others for what we have done. Fear causes us to not want to reopen old wounds and remind others of our transgressions if there is a chance they have forgotten about them. Our egos may insist we are blameless. We rationalize that if we have harmed others, it was their fault. We avoid this kind of thinking in order not to turn this step around. Step Eight is about whom we have harmed, not who has harmed us. If instead of looking at our past wrongs, we obsess about who has harmed us, we will not recover. We do not blame others but instead take responsibility for our own lives and actions. Similarly, we do not rationalize that our past wrongs should be excused because we were sick. Only by taking responsibility and making amends will we be able to put the past behind us.

Through calm, thoughtful reflection on all of our personal relationships, we gain insight about ourselves and awareness of our character defects. We can then see how we need to change. As our understanding grows, we see how the process of making amends is not so much for their sake as it is for ours. We cannot effectively change our behavior until we look at our past and consider making restitution where needed. If we are to transform our lives and become healthy, we have to be willing to clear away as much wreckage from the past as we can. We want loving, healthy relationships, so we have to start practicing the skills that are likely to foster them.

Once we have our list, we look it over to see if we are willing to make amends to everyone on it. Often, we are not. If there are some on the list to whom we feel we can make sincere amends, we do not delay and go on to Step Nine. For those whom we are not yet ready to face, we continue to strive for willingness by asking for help from our Higher Power, discussing our feelings about the situation with others, and continuing to work the program.

For this step to be successful, we need to become willing to change our behavior. True amends are made by changing the way we behave toward others. If we do not accept and forgive others as they are, we will not make amends with dignity, self-respect, and humility. In Step Nine we are going to others to make our amends; therefore, in this step we first need to forgive them. Our willingness grows as we realize not everyone needs to agree with our views. As we become more tolerant and accepting and, therefore, less rigid and judgmental, our willingness to make amends increases.

In the process of thinking about needed amends we may reopen emotional wounds. This is good, for if these feelings remain deeply buried in our minds they will inhibit our recovery. It is important for us to let go of these painful memories and the circumstances surrounding them. By taking responsibility, we will no longer continue to blame or punish ourselves. By making amends, we regain our integrity and self-worth.

We face the truth about our behavior in Step Eight. Our willingness to right our wrongs increases as we are convinced that our growth and serenity depend on our forgiveness of others and the release of old pain. We can now move on to Step Nine and begin to make amends.

STEP NINE
Made direct amends to such people wherever possible,
except when to do so would injure them or others.

In Step Nine we continue to take responsibility for our past actions. We must go to the people we have harmed and attempt to right our wrongs. There is a good reason why this step does not come sooner in the program. Since our purpose is not to cause further harm, but to improve our relationships, we must have changed sufficiently to make successful amends. This step is not meant to humiliate us, but it is necessary to free us from guilt. Through it we also forgive ourselves for our past so we can live a better life today.

MADE AMENDS
To make amends means to change or improve something or to correct an error. Making amends is not simply saying we are sorry, although an apology might be a part of an amend. We make amends by changing our behavior. We begin to act differently toward those in our lives. In making amends we try to be humble, polite, tactful, and sensible; in this way we do not become a doormat. Sometimes it requires time or money, not just words, to make amends.

If our own name is on our eighth-step list, we may have to make amends to ourselves before we go further. We have already made a beginning by coming to the program, but we make further amends to ourselves by choosing healthy patterns of living. As we work the steps, we grow in self-respect and self-esteem. We begin to accept ourselves and develop the right attitude for making amends to others.

We do not put off our amends. When we have worked Steps One through Eight we know we are ready and it is then time for action. If there is any doubt in our minds as to whether making amends to someone might cause harm to them or others, we consult a person who can give an objective opinion, perhaps a sponsor or a fifth-step person. We do not procrastinate unless there is a valid reason for delay.

We do not have to make amends for thoughts or feelings we have toward others. These really have hurt no one but ourselves, unless we have acted on them, and in that case we may owe amends. On the other hand, we do not hesitate to make amends for things which we think might seem insignificant to others. If we feel the need to make amends and are certain it will cause no harm to anyone, it has to be done for our own peace of mind.

We do not take this step in a hurry. It has to be given proper thought and planning. It does not matter where we begin. We can make the difficult amends first or the easier ones first. We need to plan where and when we will meet to avoid interruption and what we will say so as not to blame them. It is best to keep our amends simple, avoiding a great deal of explanation beyond stating what we have done that harmed them and how we intend to repair it. It is often helpful to allow some time for prayer and meditation before making amends to insure the correct outcome for everyone.

We make amends without expecting the same in return from the other person. We have to take the risk that our amends might not be accepted. Even when that does happen, we still benefit from our attempt. We know we have done what we could and so have no more need to feel guilty. We realize this amends process is more about forgiving ourselves than about receiving forgiveness from others. In most cases, however, our amends are well received and relationships are improved as people see we are consistent in our new behaviors.

We do not apologize for having gossiped about a person if there is a chance he or she is not aware of the gossip. To do so would only cause more hurt. But we can make amends by admitting to the people with whom we have shared the gossip that we were wrong to have done so. We can also strive to stop our tendency to gossip or to listen to gossip. This constitutes making indirect amends to the person we had gossiped about and direct amends to ourselves as we practice honesty and humility.

For some wrongs we may never be fully able to make amends. If we honestly know we would correct them if we could, then we can consider them taken care of. Sometimes people cannot be contacted in person because they live too far away. In that case we make our amend by sending them an honest letter of apology or making a telephone call. If people on our list are no longer living or if contacting them in person would add more damage to what was already done, we can make these amends through a fifth-step person. We can also visit the grave of the deceased and make our amends there, or write a letter as if they were still alive. Alternately, we can treat other people in the way we would have treated them if we had the opportunity to make the amends.

As we thoroughly and honestly work the program through Step Nine, we start to notice new attitudes and feelings in ourselves.

1. We realize a new freedom and happiness.

2. We do not regret the past or wish to shut the door on it.

3. We comprehend the word serenity, and we know peace of mind.

4. No matter how far down the scale we have gone, we see how our experience can benefit others.

5. The feelings of uselessness and self-pity lessen.

6. We have less concern about self and gain interest in others.

7. Self-seeking slips away.

8. Our whole attitude and outlook upon life changes.

9. Our relationships with other people improve.

10. We intuitively know how to handle situations which used to baffle us.

11. We acquire a feeling of security within ourselves.

12. We realize that God is doing for us what we could not do ourselves.*

These statements form the Twelve Promises of Emotions Anonymous. They may seem idealistic, exaggerated, or extravagant at first, but they really are possible. At our meetings we see them coming true in those around us. Some of these promises may be realized quickly, others slowly, but they will all develop naturally as a result of honestly working the EA program.

Realizing the many benefits of practicing this program, we want to maintain our growth. To do this we go on to Steps Ten, Eleven, and Twelve.

Step Ten

Continued to take personal inventory
and when we were wrong promptly admitted it.

Our lives are being transformed as we grow in self-awareness. Daily practice of the remaining steps will help us reinforce this new way of life. Although we have grown in many ways by this point, our progress toward acquiring lasting maturity and serenity will require our continued practice of the twelve-step principles. Steps One through Nine may never be completely done, and we return to them as often as necessary to continue to apply them in our daily lives. We find emotional and spiritual growth to be a lifelong process.

In doing the fourth-step inventory we dealt honestly with our past so that we could free ourselves from it. This tenth-step inventory helps

---

*Adapted from *Alcoholics Anonymous* (New York: Alcoholics Anonymous World Services, Inc., 1976), pp. 83-84.

us deal with the present as we cope with daily living. Now that we are aware of our human imperfections, we realize we can easily fall back into our old ways of thinking and behaving. With this inventory we review our day, correct our errors, accept ourselves and others, and plan ways to try to do better tomorrow. We need to be patient and persistent in doing this because our goal is progress, not perfection.

Each of us decides the best way to do our inventory. Some take their inventory in the morning and review the previous day; some take it in the evening and review that day. Some take a spot check inventory during the day when their feelings tell them it is necessary to do so. If we are hurting, we need to determine what is causing our pain. When we see conflict in our lives, we look for the character defect which is causing the problem. We then have a choice of continuing to hang onto that character defect or hurt feeling or replacing it with the opposite character asset in order to resolve the conflict.

When taking our inventory we look to see if we are setting realistic goals for ourselves. Do we acknowledge our human limitations and abilities? Are we satisfied with where we are, what we are, or what we have? Do we allow other people to be human too? Do we expect too much from others? Do we continue to rationalize our thoughts and feelings as an excuse not to accept reality? Do we utilize what we have learned in the program? Have we learned to make plans without planning the results? Do we insist on being in control?

In reviewing our day, we look for the positive things we have done and the successes we have achieved. We take stock of what our Higher Power has provided for us and take the opportunity to be grateful for it. We accept ourselves each day, whether we have done well or have slipped back into old habits. We try not to be discouraged if we fall short of our ideals. These disciplines are part of our new way of life, and we cannot expect to do them perfectly every time. We gain confidence in our new way of life by continual practice.

We continue to watch for the self-centeredness or egotism which causes our character defects. When this is evident, we ask our Higher

Power to help us be willing to have it removed. We avoid holding onto negative feelings. We cannot afford to hold on to anger, resentment, or self-pity. We avoid sulking or long silences which can result from pride or vengeance. Any of these behaviors can keep us off balance and propel us into emotional binges. We find it is pointless to be angry or resentful with people who are also suffering from the pains of being human. We are happier when we accept responsibility daily for our actions and do not fall back into the pattern of blaming others.

When we feel we have failed, we promptly admit it to ourselves and, if necessary, to others. We forgive ourselves and others. If we try and fail, at least we have tried. It is often through our failures that we learn more about ourselves. We learn not to take ourselves too seriously. We benefit by gaining a sense of humor. We find that we can laugh at ourselves.

Sometimes we find it necessary to take a more detailed inventory once or twice a year. Viewing a longer period of time allows us to see recurring situations which need our attention and to recognize our progress as we identify positive changes we have made. We can also do an inventory about a specific person or area of our lives which is causing us difficulty. This might be a family member, our job, or financial situation. By focusing only on this one area, we can often see changes we need to make, what amends are needed, and a new course of action which will bring better results for all involved.

When doing our inventory we may need to discuss things with someone to gain a clearer understanding of the situation. If we feel the need, we do this as soon as we can. When we recognize old behaviors and thinking, we attempt to stop ourselves and ask our Higher Power for help in removing them. If we feel we have harmed anyone, we make amends quickly and sincerely. An emotional slip can result if we procrastinate with any aspect of our inventory.

Through this process of continual self-appraisal we maintain our honesty and humility, we focus on living one day at a time, and we continue our progress in recovery. We realize that any measure of serenity has come to us by the grace of God. We further develop our reliance on our Higher Power in Step Eleven.

STEP ELEVEN

Sought through prayer and meditation to improve our conscious contact with God as we understood Him, praying only for knowledge of His will for us and the power to carry that out.

The Twelve Steps help us develop a partnership with the God of our understanding, no matter what image or concept we choose. In the previous steps we explored our spiritual side and established contact with a power greater than ourselves. We developed a personal understanding of this power as we surrendered our will and allowed ourselves to be guided and strengthened by our Higher Power. Step Eleven addresses our need to maintain and deepen this relationship through the use of prayer and meditation.

PRAYER

Some of us are comfortable with the idea of prayer, while others are not. Some of us pray mechanically because of fear, in times of emergency, or out of a sense of duty, while some of us doubt that God takes much interest in helping us. Others are angry with God and blame God for our illness and for the chaos in our lives. At times we try to bargain with God. We use prayer in order to get something we want from God. Sometimes our prayers are filled with bitterness and misery, as if this would gain us God's pity and favor. Step Eleven suggests we change our old ways of praying and, instead, pray for guidance and for the power to carry that out.

Prayer is talking to our Higher Power. It is being honest about the way we really feel and asking for help. We talk things over with our Higher Power as we would with a friend, and we find love and acceptance. As we establish the daily habit of prayer, we come to understand that a benefit of prayer is getting more in touch with ourselves as well as with our Higher Power. Rather than changing God, prayer changes us. It opens us to humility, patience, and the courage to face life even when life is uncertain or painful.

Many find it useful to ask their Higher Power for direction at the start of each day and to express gratitude for help received at the end of the day. In this way it becomes clearer to us who is in charge of our lives and what we need to be doing. If we sincerely seek our Higher Power's will in our lives and try to carry it out to the best of our ability, we are on the right track. If we feel unable to carry it out, the God of our understanding is a ready source of support and guidance whenever needed. All we need to do is ask.

MEDITATION

Initially, many of us have no idea what meditation is. In many ways, our past experience of focusing on pain and negativity was akin to meditation. Many of us spent days or weeks intensely concentrating on everything that was wrong with us, with our circumstances, or with other people. All we have to do now is learn to focus our attention just as fervently on the positive aspects of our lives.

Some of us are familiar with meditation but have never practiced it. Some have no idea how to go about it. Bookstores and libraries have many books about meditation which can be helpful. Some take classes on meditation techniques or go to a minister, priest, rabbi, or other spiritual advisor to learn about the traditions of meditation in particular religious faiths. In meetings we can learn as others share their methods and experiences with meditation.

Meditation can be as simple as letting our mind wander into a favorite place. It can be focusing on nature, breathing fresh air, and feeling a sense of well-being. It is letting go of our problems and negative thinking and being at peace with ourselves.

Meditation involves quieting our overactive thoughts and listening for the guidance we need. It is focused concentration. Meditation can be practiced in several ways. It can be a process of clearing our minds of all distractions so we can contemplate a spiritual truth such as love, the beauty of nature, gratitude, the unity of the universe, God, or anything positive. Many use positive statements or affirmations as the focus of meditation. The slogans and Just For Todays listed in Part III of this book can also serve this purpose. Some of us use our imagination in a positive way by incorporating specific healing images into our meditation, helping to release pain and envision new ways of being in the world today. Some use meditation as a way to relax the tension in our bodies, thereby reducing emotional and mental stress. We become refreshed mentally and physically. Whichever method we choose, the result will be improved physical, emotional, and spiritual health which allows us to cope better with daily responsibilities.

We can combine meditation and prayer into one exercise. In a quiet place we become relaxed as we contemplate a meaningful prayer or poem as the focus of our meditation. Some of us use prayers from our religious tradition or other spiritual poetry and find these to be effective for meditation. Many of us use the Serenity Prayer which very simply sums up the aim of the twelve-step program.

"God grant me the serenity to accept the things I cannot change, courage to change the things I can, and wisdom to know the difference."

As we practice Step Eleven, our ability to pray and meditate grows. As we set aside time for prayer and meditation each day, we achieve closer contact with our Higher Power. The rewards of prayer and meditation are emotional balance and a sense of belonging.

GOD'S WILL

Some of us are afraid God is going to lead us where we do not want to go. We are hesitant to surrender our destiny to an unseen Someone or Something. We fear we might lose all that we value if we give up control. We find, however, God's will does not necessarily dictate a radical change in our lives. God's will usually involves taking care of the ordinary responsibilities that are a part of everyday life so we can experience well-being. We still have free will and can choose our course of action. Experience shows us that we have more serenity if we do our best to align our will with the will of our Higher Power.

As we ask our Higher Power for guidance, we begin making better choices. If we suspect we are rationalizing or interpreting our wishful thinking as divine guidance, we consult someone with more experience and understanding in these matters. We gain confidence in our decisions as we receive added support from working this program and from other EA members.

We discover that just saying a prayer or meditating about what we cannot control brings calmness and opens us to new ways of looking at a problem. Once we see something that seems right to do and appears to be God's will for us, we take action. If there seems to be no constructive action to take, we accept that, turn the situation over to our Higher Power, and patiently await the outcome.

We may experience setbacks and crises and become doubtful about God's will for us. Sometimes it is difficult to pray or meditate, even though it is our habit to do so. We realize we have lost our spiritual connection because we have removed ourselves from our Higher Power. We can slip back into self-sufficiency as our pride and ego again struggle for control. During these difficult times, we may gain comfort and hope by asking a friend to pray with us or for us. If we persist in regular practice of prayer and meditation and accept ourselves as we are, in time the ability to pray and meditate comes back.

Power to Carry That Out

As we improve our conscious contact with the God of our understanding, we are better able to see God's will for us. We will be given the power we need to carry it out. We find that prayer and meditation makes it easier for us to handle difficult situations. We allow our will to be redirected, and, in so doing, we experience the courage and power to act according to this new direction, which is God's will.

Our partnership with God becomes a sturdy foundation which supports our daily lives. The spiritual practices we develop in this step give us direction in our new way of life. With the knowledge and tools gained in our spiritual growth, we are now ready to act in more positive ways and begin to help others in Step Twelve.

Step Twelve

Having had a spiritual awakening as the result of these steps, we tried to carry this message and to practice these principles in all our affairs.

If we have earnestly applied these steps, we have experienced profound changes. Through this program we have evolved into new and better people. By being willing to risk self-examination, being open and honest with others, and surrendering to our Higher Power, we have grown personally and achieved a level of recovery. We no longer feel alone. We are connected to a spiritual source of strength and serenity. Through this spiritual awakening we are being restored to sanity.

Spiritual Awakening

A spiritual awakening is the gift we receive after working the first eleven steps. It happens as we become aware of and develop our spiritual nature. We each experience it in different ways since our individual journeys through the steps have been different from anyone else's. Some people experience a sudden, dramatic spiritual awakening. They are inspired with a deep certainty that God exists, and they feel profound gratitude for their newly found faith. For most, personal enlightenment is a more subtle process as the steps are applied and changes are realized. A spiritual awakening can be awareness and acceptance of how little power we really have, while at the same time we can feel a greater sense of well-being, self-respect, and self-esteem. It can be the realization that no matter how poorly we have behaved in the past, we are worthwhile people. It can be a recognition that people are available, not to threaten us, but to support us. It can be the reassurance that we have a Higher Power who will help us. It can include a feeling of being connected to life, of being whole rather than disjointed and alienated. It can be the realization that the promises of the program are coming true for us or a feeling of gratitude for all we have received.

Whatever form it may take, our awakening contains a characteristic attitude change. We have become less obsessed with our problems and pain and more open to other people. If we once suffered addictive or compulsive behaviors, these are greatly diminished or gone altogether. We are willing to participate in life and want to contribute our talents wherever we can do good. We are glad to share with others what we have learned.

CARRY THIS MESSAGE

We learn that sharing our progress and encouraging others brings us more understanding and growth. A paradox of the program is that to keep what we have learned for ourselves, we must give it away. With some degree of recovery resulting from practicing these steps, we can begin to reach out to others and share what we have learned. We share our stories — what we used to be like, what happened as we worked the steps, and how we have changed. This sharing allows us to see our experiences in a new light, and, consequently, we learn more about ourselves. By sharing we can more clearly see all the changes we have made and realize other ways to apply these principles in our lives. This strengthens our commitment to use the program. We share our experience, strength, and hope with people to give them the opportunity to change their lives by this avenue of recovery.

Some of us, in our enthusiasm and excitement early in our recovery, try to get everyone we know to join EA. We know many people in our lives who we think need to change and should be in this program. They usually resist joining or are resentful of our suggestions. We then feel hurt and misunderstood. People are usually not receptive if we try to preach the program, and, as we gain experience in carrying the message of EA, we realize how arrogant it is to think we should point out to others their need for this program. It is far better for us to share the program with those who want it than with those we think need it. Carrying the message is part of our recovery; it is not about saving other people. We only share our experiences and try not to control the outcome. With this in mind, we feel less disappointment when others do not accept our message. We need to remember that the efforts are ours, but the results come from God.

We find many ways to do twelfth-step work. One important way is by example. We demonstrate that this program works through what we do in our lives. People see how we are recovering and want to know what we are doing. Some members invest time and energy into service activities that benefit their groups and EA as a whole. Some have a talent for speaking about the program or sharing their stories. Others are less visible in their efforts, but just as valuable to the functioning of their groups. Everyone has something to contribute. Anyone can begin working this part of Step Twelve in small ways very early in the program and thus, experience the rewards of being involved in the EA community.

Some ways we can carry this message are:

1. Attending meetings and sharing with others.
2. Helping new people feel welcome before and after meetings.
3. Setting up the meeting room and cleaning up afterwards.
4. Taking time to listen to someone on the telephone.
5. Taking responsibility for collecting group donations, ordering literature, or paying the bills for the group.
6. Helping others discover the best ways for them to understand and work the Twelve Steps.
7. Making personal contributions to assure that our group, intergroup, and the International Service Center continue to provide needed services.
8. Starting new groups and supporting other groups that are having difficulties.
9. Writing articles for the *The New Message* magazine.
10. Holding public information meetings, doing mailings, or distributing flyers to let others know about EA.

11. Speaking about the twelve-step program.

12. Serving on committees, in intergroup, or on the International Service Board of Trustees.

PRACTICE THESE PRINCIPLES

By working these steps, we are integrating many new principles into our lives. Some of these principles are acceptance, honesty, open-mindedness, willingness, patience, humility, compassion, courage, selflessness, and spirituality. In reality, none of us may ever master these principles perfectly, but they give us ideals to strive toward. After we have been in the program for some time, these principles become second nature to us.

Each of us creates our own daily plan for practicing the Twelve Steps. We need to continue using the whole program, not just choosing the easier steps. If we avoid the spiritual parts of the program, or if we skip over steps that still seem too fearful or difficult, we are not working the whole program. When this is the case the program will not work, and we are not likely to continue our recovery. This twelve-step program only works for us when we choose to work it.

If we become complacent about using the program, we often find that our old thoughts, attitudes, and behaviors return. It seems our illness, like alcoholism, is only arrested, not cured. We experience emotional slips if we do not use what we have learned. We have to use the principles of the program diligently for as long as we want recovery. When we experience a slip, and many of us do, we take action to bring our program into focus again. We look for the part of the program that we have stopped doing or that we have stopped doing well. We use the tools of the program — meetings, phone calls, slogans, Just for Todays, EA literature, the steps, inventories, prayer, and meditation — to return to practicing the principles. We once again participate in our recovery. Our emotional and spiritual fitness allow us to meet the challenges of life in appropriate ways. We are able to turn challenges into opportunities as we demonstrate our faith — faith in our Higher Power and faith in this twelve-step program.

IN ALL OUR AFFAIRS

This is a program about living a new way of life. We do not just talk about it once a week at meetings. It is a program for living well twenty-four hours a day wherever we are. Because we are changing as a result of these steps, we find ourselves beginning to use these program principles in all aspects of our lives. We are more caring, honest, and accepting with all the people in our lives, not just with EA people. As we recover our emotional health and are restored to sanity, the dysfunction in our homes and families is often reduced. We apply our new principles in our social lives and enjoy improved relationships. We discover that acting from the foundation of the twelve-step program in our business or professional lives makes us better employees or employers. In our financial matters we are more balanced, neither miserly nor reckless. EA principles become our guidelines for thinking, so our mental health is improved. We take better care of our physical and emotional needs. We now feel the security of knowing we have available to us the spiritual resources of a personal Higher Power, and we have a concept of God that works for us.

Many of us choose to continue attending meetings, even though we now have lives so much better than our old ones. Long-term membership helps us maintain what we have learned and helps us continue to grow. We remember where we were and what we were like before the program. We have received a great gift by the grace of God. We continue to serve others in EA as an expression of gratitude for what we have received. We remember that someone was here to support us when we first came to EA, and we want to insure the program will be available to anyone who wants it.

PART II

Personal Stories

These stories are the personal experiences of Emotions Anonymous members, told in their own words, about how they found recovery in this program. We believe these stories demonstrate the variety of reasons why people have come to EA and the success they have had. Since we are experts only on our own stories, no one is speaking for EA as a whole. Because in EA we believe no one is more important than another, the stories have been arranged in random order.

COME FLY WITH US

Doris

I am a very different person than I was when I found the program almost eight years ago. Before EA I was an empty shell, and, yet, I thought I knew it all. I thought if I just figured out how to fix everybody else I would be happy. Since EA, I have learned that I know very little. I now leave other people alone to make their own mistakes and to win their own victories. I am working on trying to fix the only person I can, me. I recently graduated from the State University with honors, and I am currently in graduate school. My goal is to be a therapist. I know first hand that without mental and emotional well-being we have no life at all. The brilliant insights and wisdom of those early EA members who were here when I got here have allowed me to learn a healthy way of life (have actually allowed me to live a life) beyond my highest expectations. The thirty or so people whom I have sponsored over the years have also inspired me, with their honest and courageous actions, to grow along with them. I will always be indebted to my first sponsor, who showed me God. I am a miracle of this program and living proof that the steps work. I am a real person today.

When I came into the program I was thirty years old and ready to die. I didn't know who I was. I had been drinking since I was thirteen and drugging since I was sixteen. I had my first death wish at age twelve and tried to kill myself, but I was too scared to jump off the pier. I sat on that pier half the night, crying and praying for an end to my miserable life. I tried again when I was fifteen. That time I took seventeen downers, wrote half a dozen good-bye notes and was astonished to wake up the next day and find that it hadn't worked. I was supposed to be dead! In my stupor, I dressed for school and actually made it there but was sent to the nurse's office on suspicion of being high. The hopelessness of that moment still tugs at my heart. I never felt more misunderstood. Of course, I denied being high. I wasn't high; I was suicidal, but they never knew that. They just let me sleep it off until it was time to go home.

My third and most serious suicide attempt was at age twenty-four. My drug-addicted husband had beaten me for the hundredth time — punching me and kicking me until I was half-senseless. My two babies were sleeping peacefully in their cribs. I went into my bedroom and swallowed the remainder of my new tranquilizer prescription — about twenty-four pills. I woke up in the intensive care unit three days later. I couldn't believe it. I had failed again.

That attempt left me with substantial memory losses. Ironically, I lost those parts of my memory which had given me some measure of pleasure and self-esteem. I remembered being a good singer, but I forgot how to sing, and I forgot all the songs. I remembered being a gourmet cook, but I forgot how to make even the most basic meal. I remembered being competent in several other areas but could no longer function in any of them. I withdrew into myself even more than before. I began to develop phobias — especially answering the phone, answering the door, or going out. Only with daily use of marijuana and beer could I function at all.

I went in and out of depression for the next six years and the thought of suicide never left me. I tried everything I could think of to help myself, to improve myself, when I had the energy. I wanted so much to be normal and, especially, to be happy. I tried going to church, going to school, going to the gym, going to the beach, drinking less, not drinking, reading self-improvement books, listening to inspirational tapes, attending motivational seminars, and taking trips. I tried nutrition, kinky sex with my husband, community involvement, psychiatrists, psychologists, counselors, crime, violence, avoiding my parents, seeing my parents, working, not working, being sweet and docile, being a raging maniac . . . and nothing ever made me feel better for long. In fact, most of these extreme behavior shifts exhausted me and sent me back into depression. I hated myself so much.

Eventually, I just hung on for my babies who were getting bigger every year. I felt that I would live until they could fend for themselves, and then I would kill myself and get it over with once and for all. I was so sick and out of touch that I thought my children would be able to handle losing their mother to suicide when they reached ages six and seven.

The year my children reached six and seven I had a nervous breakdown. I didn't have another suicide attempt in me. I just retreated from the world, from my family, and from my life. In a bizarre re-creation of that lonely night spent crying and praying on the end of a pier, I cried and ranted and raved for twelve excruciating days. I spent some of the time on the bathroom floor, begging God to help me, asking why God wouldn't help me. But most of the time I was in bed with the pillows and the covers over my head alternately sleeping and crying. I had reached that awful impasse of being too afraid to live and too afraid to die. Having tried everything to help myself, and having failed, I had reached the bottom. I was thirty years old, and I had wasted my life. I felt worthless, despicable, ugly, and helpless.

At that time I had very little understanding of my situation and no awareness at all of why I ended up emotionally and mentally shattered by age thirty. I thought there was something intrinsically wrong with me. I thought I was a bad person because I could not overcome these problems on my own. I now know better than that. I now know I am a good person, and that God does not make junk.

As a last ditch effort to find some measure of relief from the pain and constant disorientation that plagued me, I went to my first EA meeting. I found the people there to be attractive, funny, welcoming, and amazingly honest. Why, this bunch talked about feelings of jealousy, hatred, anger, frustration, anxiety, and depression as if these were normal topics of conversation! They made it look so easy. Here was a group of people who were talking openly about all my secrets and shameful feelings. They had them too! It was quite a revelation. For the first time in my life, I felt real hope. I was not alone!

I began working the steps after attending meetings for about six months. My sponsor directed me to get a better perspective on my childhood, so my first real inventory was of my childhood, of what was done to me.

My grandfather died about six weeks before I was born. Though his death had nothing to do with me, I believe now that his dying at that particular time probably saved my life. My grandmother, bound by a death-bed promise to never wed again, sold her home and all her belongings and came to live with us in our little two bedroom rowhouse in Philadelphia. She was still young and beautiful, and she was willing to take care of me and my older sister, who was one and a half, so my mother could go to work full-time. My grandmother took care of the house and the cooking and sewing and did all the things for us that mothers do for their children. Everyone who saw us assumed she was our mother.

My father and mother, both products of Hitler's Germany and both traumatized by World War II, became workaholics. Neither of them had any time or energy for their two little girls except to lecture and punish in large measure. Every Sunday after church we were told about how great Hitler was. It always started with a headline from the newspaper about some mugging or murder or robbery which, according to my father, was proof that the United States needed a Hitler too. I cannot count how many times I heard my father begin a family lecture with, "If only Hitler were running this country ... ." In those Sunday talks, my father would advocate mass public hangings, mutilations, and torture of law-breakers. My mother quietly agreed.

My father had a violent temper — we lived in constant fear when he was around. Like many other members of EA, I suffered a lot of physical and emotional abuse disguised as punishment for things that were really just mistakes or fumbles. I remember when I was four, I was told to set the table. For some reason, my father was already seated at the table and was watching me carefully to make sure I did it right. I was so scared and self-conscious that I dropped the last plate in my hand which would have been the plate at his place. He beat me severely about the head and torso, called me names, accused me of deliberately breaking the plate, declared me unfit to be in his presence, and sent me to my room without food or water or bathroom privileges for a day. Scenes like that were common occurrences in our house. No one was safe.

When I was very young, I remember that my mother tried to be loving toward us, but, as I got older, she grew colder. When she lost her temper, her rage didn't fit the situation. She would go berserk over things that weren't that bad, and her rage didn't burn off for a couple of days. She hit us with hangers, broom handles, vacuum cleaner extensions, and any other weapons that were handy. By the time I was a teenager, she was slapping me hard in the face on a daily basis. The last bad beating I took from her was when I was twenty-six. I couldn't escape her then because I had a broken collar bone. I thought she hated me.

There, in the midst of so much pain and violence and humiliation, was my grandmother. She shielded us as much as she could and compensated with unconditional love, good humor, and generosity. She probably saved my life just by being there. I was twenty-three when she died from injuries sustained in a car accident. I didn't know it then, but I lost the only person who cared about me. By that time I was so wrapped up in a self-destructive lifestyle, I was incapable of feeling my grief for her death. I felt nothing except an all consuming hatred of my parents. I never appreciated my grandmother when she was alive. I took her for granted. Only the trauma of my parents' violence was real to me. I had become addicted to violence and addicted to pain. In spite of my best efforts, I just didn't know the way out.

My marriage was in many ways a continuation of my childhood pain. I tried to make it work in spite of incredible emotional, physical, and sexual abuse. I blamed myself for many of our problems. After all,

I was depressed and paranoid so much, and I had no self-esteem. I couldn't really blame him for the way he treated me nor was I capable of leaving him and being independent. However, Emotions Anonymous changed all that.

I worked the steps continuously. I turned my will and my life over to the care of God, as I understood God. I became of service to others and, eventually, spreading the message of the Twelve Steps became more important to me than reviewing my own miseries. After one final marital humiliation, I threw my husband out and filed for divorce. The loving support I received in meetings during that terrifying and torturous period carried me through to freedom. I made amends to all the people who had suffered because of my illness, and I paid my debts. I forgave my parents because, first, they can't really hurt me anymore and, second, because hating them was hurting me. I am slowly building a relationship with my father based on mutual honesty and respect. This is a gift of the program which was never possible before I worked the steps. Sadly, my mother remains unapproachable. The program has taught me that in EA all things are possible, so I will leave that relationship in God's hands for now. My children have also benefitted from EA. They love having a reasonable, rational, trustworthy mother. The younger one asked me once to promise I would never stop going to meetings.

The members of EA are now my new family. They care for me in times of illness. They comfort me in times of trouble. They lend me their strength when I haven't enough of my own. I am often reminded of a story I heard at a meeting. It compares us to a flock of geese flying south for the winter. When a goose flaps its wings, it creates an uplift for the goose immediately behind it. By flying in a V-formation, the flock can travel more than twice as far than if each goose traveled on its own. When the lead goose gets tired, it falls back in formation and another leads for a while until it gets tired. The geese in the back honk to encourage those in the front to keep up their speed. When a goose, for whatever reason, drops out of the V, it feels the drag and resistance of trying to go it alone. It works very hard to rejoin the group in order to take advantage of the lifting power of the goose in front of it.

Being in EA is like that. I quickly learned that life's journey is much harder and slower when I try to go it alone. I need the uplift of the others in my group. I need the encouragement and the rotation of leadership. I have a long way to go on my new adventure, but with the love and support of my EA family, I am likely to go twice as far as I ever could on my own.

At Peace

Cassa

The first significant event I remember was being told I was adopted. My parents read me a story about a boy named Penny who was adopted and how he was wanted twice. Then they said this was to be a secret, and we would never discuss this subject again. Even at five years of age, I had questions which were not to be answered.

I was a *busy* child, probably what would be called hyperactive today. I was a thumb sucker, a nail biter, at age eight an overeater, and a smoker at thirteen. I had vast amounts of energy and no idea how to use it constructively. I learned in this program that I was addicted to my own adrenalin.

We were a military family and moved a great deal. I remember not feeling a part of, or connected with, anything or anyone. My father spent three years in Europe during World War II. He fell in love with an English woman. I always felt he would have asked for a divorce, but my mother became pregnant. His affair became an ever-growing cancer in our family. My father turned to alcohol and became very quiet and withdrawn. My mother never forgot and never let him forget. The tension and outbursts of anger kept us all on pins and needles. I became the peacemaker; my sister the overachiever. My father took his life at age eighty-seven to escape from his wife.

My mother's messages, "You don't need to get married, having a career is more important" and "Don't trust men," are deeply buried in me as a belief system. I have always picked men who made her belief correct. I put two fingers on my head as if they are radar and know I will hone right in on a man that cannot be trusted. Even being aware of this does not always mean I can change, but I feel I have a much better understanding of the choices I have made, and I am hopeful that my future decisions will bring greater happiness.

When I found Emotions Anonymous, I had been attending A.A. meetings with my best friend. I wanted what those people had. I told them I would go drink so I could qualify. They said I was crazy. I wanted to stop the world and get off. Their program was my last resort. Then one night an A.A. member suggested I try Emotions Anonymous.

My first EA meeting was like coming home. They were talking about the same feelings I had. They also had the Twelve Steps, Twelve Traditions, slogans, and an additional gift, the Just For Todays. I found a positive framework within which to live. I chose a sponsor to help me work the steps and with whom I could share. For the first time in my life I had support, acceptance, and unconditional love from my Higher Power, my sponsor, and those EA members. They were able to give me the acceptance my family could not give. They loved and accepted me when I felt unlovable and unacceptable.

Shortly after joining EA, I decided to try and work on acceptance of a co-worker. We couldn't stand each other. It was far from easy for me to let this person be who he was and not react or try to change him. About six months later, I was transferred to another department. I said my goodbyes to this co-worker and knew I was different. I learned that each situation is an opportunity to live my program and to grow. I realized that this program is a situation by situation opportunity. Each opportunity is there for me to learn and change.

I am grateful to all who came before me and to those who had success stories to share. They gave me hope that this simple program could change my life. Today I am different. I am comfortable in my own skin.

Both of my parents passed away within the last three years. I was able to work Steps Eight and Nine (making amends) with both of them. My father took fifteen minutes. He told me about his affair, that it was true. I told him I only felt sadness for him for all the years he had lived with my mother's rage. I told him I loved him, that I had not been the greatest daughter, and I knew I had caused him grief. He said he didn't remember that. It was a powerful fifteen minutes, and I recognized we were both at peace with each other.

My amends to my mother took five years. First, I had to become trustworthy. If I said I would do something, I had to do it. I spent time with her every week. I treated my mother the way I wanted her to treat me. During her last year, she suffered extensive memory loss. She forgot why she was angry, and she became kinder.

When my parents died there was no guilt, nothing left undone or unsaid. I was free. This is one of the greatest gifts the program has given me. This program helps me understand what I must do to live at peace with myself, not what others need to do for me.

The steps are in a specific order for a reason. The first three steps help me see I am powerless and that I need a Higher Power. I have the opportunity to really look at what kind of Higher Power I have and see if I can surrender my will and my life to that Higher Power. Steps Four and Five, doing the inventory and sharing it, help me tell the truth to myself and to another person. I realize what my character defects are and ask for help in Steps Six and Seven. I improve my relationships with others by making amends in Steps Eight and Nine. In Steps Ten, Eleven, and Twelve I review my day with an inventory, seek my Higher Power for guidance and friendship, and help others.

How blessed I feel to have found this wonderful program. It is almost like knowing a secret — a secret way to live. I thank my Higher Power for all the pain. Without the pain I would not have been searching for help. I am proud to say to anyone that I am a member of Emotions Anonymous. Keep coming back!

Anxiety Got My Attention

Bill

I tried many ways to fit into daily living. As a youth, I tried to use good manners and be seen and not heard. I got the message that I was full of potential, and I should excel. I also got the message that my opinions were not important, decisions would be made for me, and whatever they were, that would be that.

I was sheltered, actually smothered, by a parent who was probably never allowed to grow up emotionally herself. She had a child and did her best. I believe my mother's fear was transmitted to me while I was still in the womb. My safety and the term *Be Careful* have haunted my life for as long as I can remember. In my life *Be Careful* translated into chronic anxiety. From the beginning I felt like a normal boy, but I was kept hidden from the truth by a lifelong sequence of secrets. I didn't know I was being kept a prisoner from reality, and I proceeded to walk through life without the balance that occurs when you see, hear, and recognize the realities of life. I felt as though something harmful was going to happen, and I had done something to cause the shame and guilt-laden feelings.

I became alcoholic, and my addictive traits grew. I developed hypochondria and many phobias. Three co-dependent marriages in twelve years did not provide me with the surrogate parent I was seeking. My instability and chronic worry became my constant companions prior to my introduction to the Twelve Steps.

An earlier diagnosis of schizophrenia became a chronic anxiety problem. I tried suicide or thought of it as a way out as often as twice a day on occasion. I had many years of therapy, have been locked up in mental health facilities, and have attended crisis groups.

My history includes twenty-plus years of alcoholism, a severe addiction to downers including Valium, phenobarbital, seconal and, finally, anything at all. I was on state disability and social security disability aid to the totally disabled. I was pronounced unable to care for my own affairs. Due to my chemical and substance abuse, I was given less than a year to live. I had resigned myself to a fast approaching end to my life.

My step-daughter, Cynthia, who had to endure my alcoholism and lifelong neurotic behavior, was the twelve-step angel for me to find a new way of life. I began to attend Alcoholics Anonymous meetings and did so for twelve years. I made progress and my life changed, thanks to the God I found.

My chronic anxiety never left even after I got sober. I had to begin a search in sobriety for help with my emotional upheavals.

After twelve years in the original twelve-step program of A.A., my anxiety level raised to a point that required additional attention — another surrender. I looked in the newspaper for a self-help group that could benefit a twelve year A.A. member. I prayed and talked with others in the hope of getting some direction.

A short time later, after a meeting a long-time member asked how it was going. This allowed me to share that I was having emotional upheavals even though I was grateful for twelve years of sobriety. He told me his return of dysfunctional behavior had caused him to search for additional direction. He suggested Emotions Anonymous. A coincidence like that is a complicated way of saying God.

I attended my first EA meeting and within ten minutes I heard that I was powerless over my emotions. I had thought it and maybe said it before, but the awareness came as I sat among those who acknowledged that fact on a regular basis. At first I was unable to relax. I felt frozen and stiff, my negative emotions had hold of me. However, I believe I was given the Twelve Steps for tense times, and the simple manner these steps offer give me the ability to face life on life's terms.

Jealousy disqualified me because I believed I didn't count in life as much as other people. Today I consider EA to stand for Emotions Anonymous and in my story it means Equal Adult, aware of my own worth.

Diminished fears have bolstered my confidence. Fear has not left me totally, but it occupies a much smaller territory. Calling on the Serenity Prayer is a large part of my spiritual growth. My new willingness to compromise has shown me that my former stubbornness was a reversal of H – honesty, O – open-mindedness, and W – willingness. The HOW of "How it Works."

I tried to solve my emotional problems by self-indulgence and it did not work. It does not work today either. Step Seven, "Humbly asked Him to remove our shortcomings," reminds me of early teachings which I balked at "I, of myself, am nothing; the Father doeth the works." Today I see that it is true.

God, as I understand Him, has been understanding in my struggles within the framework of the Twelve Steps. When I started the steps I was a beginner, and I am able to redo the steps as needed. When having difficult periods, I can go to the prior step or begin again with progress as my goal, not perfection. I enjoy attending step-study meetings. I go to participation meetings to participate in my own recovery. I share and listen and care, sometimes I just occupy a chair. I consider this to be my twelfth-step work.

By forgiving rather than being resentful, I can initiate the healing of our fellowship. Acceptance has replaced my constant condemning. I was taught that when I point a judgmental finger at you, three of my own fingers will be pointing in my direction.

I believe that being powerless over one's emotions is the ultimate surrender. We all have emotions and seldom are we given the opportunities to acknowledge powerlessness as a growing tool to be applied to our lives.

I recently participated in a Twelve Step Day in the Southern California area. As I stood and faced the men and women of EA, I saw a divine mirror of love, acceptance, and tolerance. I was never told I didn't belong or that I wasn't wanted. They opened their EA arms that day as they did at my first meeting.

I am grateful today in contrast to the self-pity that prevailed for years. Thanks to the program, I can look for the good and find it most of the time. I can lose a job or a relationship and feel the emotions involved, but there is a positive side to all situations when I apply the practical tools of the slogans found in our EA literature.

Emotions Anonymous was waiting for me, and I was looking for Emotions Anonymous. I didn't know it until anxiety got my attention. God took my hand, and Emotions Anonymous welcomed me home. Thanks to all of you.

I Did the Footwork

Cathy

Having three older brothers and three older sisters, I was able to use my family name to get through school. I now know I was not stupid; however, I was a failure because I was afraid to risk. Having emotional, physical, and spiritual illness, the world was always slightly out of focus. Each new situation seemed more formidable to me than it actually was. In short, I had perfected the art of negative thinking, and this tendency, although lessened, did not immediately vanish by working the Twelve Steps of recovery.

After years of therapy, I was told I wouldn't be able to function in the outside world for more than twelve to sixteen months at a time. I would always need a controlled hospital within that period. From shock treatments I will always have difficulty with my memory. Doctors said not to worry about being addicted to medication as I always would need it to be a functional human being. They also warned about not being able to have close relationships.

Then I found the twelve-step program. In the beginning I heard "Keep coming back. If you work the Twelve Steps here are promises that will happen in your life." Whew! Broken promises; it's okay, I was used to them.

Members talked to me, and they didn't even know my family. When will they ask me to leave? Do they really care? How can they say they are depressed and laugh? That kept me coming back.

There was never anything wrong with my intelligence. It was my emotions which were sick. I always had worked in severe depression, anxiety, and fear. I didn't know it then, but I was practicing "Bring the body, the head will follow." As I look back, I wonder how I ever found the courage to get up in the morning, but get up I did. There was only one thing I was really sure of — there was no way to go but up. Even my suicide attempts were like jumping out of a basement window, they weren't working either.

The Emotions Anonymous meetings I attended talked of getting a sponsor. It was the best gift I gave myself. For the first time, other than in closed doors with a therapist, I shared.

My sponsor listened; I learned. She guided; I learned. She listened; I took action. We became best friends. With growth came opportunity, and the impossible became possible. My sponsor shared with me that if I wanted to recover, not just feel better, I must do the Twelve Steps. Here are some of the things I learned.

Step One: It was necessary to admit I am powerless over my emotions, to admit without any reservations whatsoever and accept it, to recognize my state of neurosis. Then I started surrendering. I found it was not a weakness to surrender completely. Over a period of time I felt a power and strength I never knew existed. The results were proportional to the degree I surrendered. I let my guard down, and I started listening and stopped debating. The only thing I found that was important was application and my degree of applying.

Step Two: The words "came to believe" imply it took time. I gradually acquired a belief in a Higher Power to restore me. Going to meetings helped bring this about. Sharing my experience was the true therapy of my program. If I was going to be comfortable, I must come to believe in a Power greater than myself. Willpower was not a factor in recovery until the compulsion had been removed. Believing in a Power greater than myself restored me to sane behavior.

Step Three: This step let me correct my illness under God's supervision. I learned that when I made a decision, I did not take action on it. It's important for me to believe in a Power greater than myself and to rely on it. Rely in every aspect of life, this gets the self out. My ego was hard to overcome. As I turned my life over to God, I began to get rid of my ego. My life started changing when I had faith along with a reliance on my Higher Power. I must keep practicing turning my life over to God. Choice followed by responsible actions made the difference.

Step Four: With this step I broke new ground and began exciting, new ventures. I learned I am a product of my past, but I do not have to remain a victim of my past. My sponsor suggested I write down everything good, bad, or indifferent that impressed me from as far back as I could remember. Then I was to try not analyzing it in any way or taking anyone else's inventory. It helped me to keep my mind on the purpose of my inventory, which was to get out all the garbage and straighten out my life. I was surprised to remember my early Christmas time when Santa did come, and also the family picnics at Coney Island. The defects of character I found could be changed to assets. My sponsor kept saying "nobody died from learning about themselves."

Step Five: After I "cleaned house" by doing the inventory, I was ready to grow. This was the beginning of the true ingredients of this program. Having gotten rid of the garbage, I felt like a great sheet of steel had been lifted. I had new energy added to my life. My sponsor suggested once I got the garbage out to leave it out, so I quit living in the past. I didn't dwell on the inventory. I didn't dwell on tomorrow either. Today was all I had with which to concern myself. I felt great relief and got rid of the inner turmoil. In our original EA book it said, "Immediately following the fifth step, it is well to find a quiet place and carefully review what transpired, thanking God for allowing us to know Him better."

Step Six: Steps One through Five helped me to work in the right direction as I built my foundation for ultimate surrender. In Step Six I confronted the need to change my attitudes and lifestyle. As my willingness to surrender increased, the more I invited my Higher Power to lead my journey. With my sponsor's guidance I listed my character defects from my inventory.

Step Seven: Humility is a recurring theme in the twelve-step program and the central idea of Step Seven. To me, humility means honesty. I got on my knees and asked God to remove each shortcoming individually. As I gave up my shortcomings, I was surrendering. Every change in my life lifted me to a new level of understanding.

Step Eight: To make amends does not mean to say "I'm sorry." To me it means something is wrong with our relationship, and I am willing to be responsible for my part. I made a list which including my own name. I also included the names of people I felt I had harmed. I needed to become willing to take the responsibility for my actions, to be willing to make amends.

Step Nine: I needed to pay back money which was taken. I did this through a charity. I had moved three thousand miles from my family, and it became important to go back and show them I was leading a life of freedom. I had made positive choices. I had to be willing to make amends as long as no one involved would be hurt. The Twelve Promises are at the end of Step Nine. At this time EA was the only stability in my life. The promises did come true. As this step became a reality for me, I found I was the only thinker in my mind. I belonged as an equal because I felt like one of God's kids for the first time. I started handling my experiences with wisdom, love, and ease.

Step Ten: The tenth step is a way of keeping my house clean and in order. The EA book tells us there are three types of inventories — life inventory, daily inventory, and spot check inventory. When I have an emotional upheaval, I had to learn to stop — stop immediately and take a spot check inventory. I say the Serenity Prayer and think the situation through. In the daily inventory I ask myself at the end of the day did anxiety or fear enter into my thinking? Did I become emotionally upset? If so, have I laid my faith aside? I ask myself if I was honest and aboveboard in all my conversations and dealings? Did I lead anyone to believe anything that wasn't right or true? I wake each morning and confirm I need to carry a grateful attitude. I found I could not be unhappy and grateful at the same time. I must be aware of my thinking, but this took lots of discipline. My understanding became clearer, and I was willing to change.

Step Eleven: When I pray I talk to God. When I meditate I listen to God. I ask God for inspiration and guidance. I give thanks to God for the guidance and blessings that are part of the day. The fruits of the eleventh step are that I am never alone. I never have that deadly alone feeling that I was so used to. I began to grow more and more emotionally stable. I began to face reality in everyday living as it actually was. As I became emotionally mature it was easier to accept anything that came my way. I don't fight with myself anymore. This was a start of maturity. I began to accept healing miracles in my life and in my world.

Step Twelve: This step gave my illness a purpose. Helping to make someone else's pain easier helps me. Action is the magic word. When I help another, I can't wallow in self-pity. When all else fails, this works. Whatever I want in life, all I have to do is give it away. I am limited only by my own capacity to give. I had to learn to share with others what I had been given. This, for me, is the twelfth step. I had the need to be needed. The more I love myself, the more I love others. The more love I give, the more love I have to give.

Since being in EA, I have not needed to be hospitalized. After four years in the program, I was off all medication. I had held the same job for eighteen years when I risked changing careers. After doing my ninth step, I met my prince charming. We dated a year and a half, lived together a year and a half, and our seventeenth wedding anniversary will be in a few months. I am okay with all members of my family. With my family of choice, EA, I have a support system that helps me daily.

It has not been easy. It took many years for me to get where I am today. Today, as doors open, I walk in and risk. This is a long way from the child I was.

I retain the right to have problems, to cry, to make mistakes, and to not have all the answers. I attend meetings. I still use a sponsor. I continue to take inventories. I seek through prayer and meditation to improve my conscious contact with God, and service is my way of life. I accept and surrender my will and life every day.

For twenty-three years twelve-step programs have been a way of life. I am okay today. I am a miracle. EA is special — it's a hug wherever I am. I'm grateful for all who touched my life in recovery. I did the footwork; God gave me the results. Love and hugs to you all.

No Longer a Victim

Christina

Depression is a gray mass of fog
on which the "puzzle of life" is sitting.
Suddenly, and without warning,
everything is ripped apart,
and I feel myself falling.
The arms of fear are coming closer,
twisting and tangling themselves around me
while my lifeless form continues falling
into a state of nothingness.
The fear then becomes a massive gray wall.
My exhausted mind frantically searches
for a way over it, under it, or around it,
but it is hopeless.
I am trapped.
I am out of control, unable to breathe,
and completely paralyzed.
I can hear my heart beating against my chest,
and I want to scream over and over again,
but my voice remains silent.
Of the millions of people,
no one hears my cry, and there I remain,
left alone to wither and die unknown and unloved.
Thus the unending cycle of life and death
continues with steadfast purpose.

My name is Christina, and I'm powerless over my emotions. As I look back on my life, I can see that I have always had emotional problems, and feeling "down" was just how I was.

My childhood was filled with an alcoholic father, two abusive step-fathers, and a mother trapped by her own fear. I was sexually and mentally abused. My second step-father constantly told me, "I'm watching and waiting, and one of these days you're going to mess up, and when you do I'll be there." I was afraid of everyone and trusted no one.

I spent a lot of time daydreaming in order to avoid my memories and emotions. As the years went by I fell into a pattern of depression, suicidal thoughts, abusive relationships, panic attacks, anorexia, and satanic nightmares. I hit bottom when I discovered I had cancer. I was going to die, and I hadn't even lived.

I had been introduced to EA several years earlier, but had rejected it because, as a victim, I felt I didn't owe amends to anyone. They owed me amends. Church, therapy, and books said a lot, but never answered the big question of how. They didn't seem to have any tools or directions. I wasn't sure what I was looking for, but I knew I was dying inside. I had already been in therapy for several years, had spent a month in a psychiatric hospital, and had tried many religious denominations. Nothing had worked. I was desperate enough to try anything that offered hope. I was lonely and miserable, and EA was offering me a guarantee. They guaranteed to return my misery if I didn't find recovery. What did I have to lose? It has been four years now, and I am a different person. I am a survivor, not a victim.

My recovery started with the first three steps which I will paraphrase: I can't; God can; I think I'll let him. I felt God had pretty much messed up my life already, and I wasn't sure I wanted to trust Him again. But then I hadn't done such a good job on my own either, and I had to do something.

The slogans "You are not alone" and "I have a choice" were news to me! I could say *no* without feeling guilty. I didn't have to let people walk all over me. I could do whatever I needed to do for myself, and it wasn't selfish. It was healthy. When I took a good honest look at Step Four, I discovered I had brought on many of my problems myself.

From doing this inventory I could see I definitely wasn't a saint, but then neither was I a monster. I had some character defects and some character assets.

Through Steps Five, Six, and Seven, along with a lot of talking, writing, and praying, I have begun to live and believe in myself again. I have a pretty good relationship with my Higher Power most of the time. I still ask *why* often and let Him know when I don't agree with Him, but that's okay.

I have worked the rest of the steps on some of my problems and have gone back to the beginning of the steps with others. At first I thought I would do all the steps and be through, but I found I have to work the steps completely with each individual situation.

I found the *Just for Todays* to be a great help in the early days, when getting out of bed was a major accomplishment. I still keep them within easy reach as I am now getting out in the world and doing things.

I have gone back to school to fulfill my dream of one day being a paramedic. I am taking a self-defense class and singing in the church choir. I am eating and sleeping better. I am off all tranquilizers. My cancer is in remission. My husband has his wife back and my children have their mom back.

Did EA *do* this for me? No one person or thing could do it for me. I had to do it for myself. I had to read the literature, go to meetings, talk, talk, and talk some more. I had to accept what could not be changed (my past), had the courage to change what could be changed (myself), and learned the difference.

So what *did* EA do? The members accepted me without question. They made EA literature available and provided transportation when needed. They were not afraid to tell me to "take the cotton out of my ears and put it in my mouth" when needed. They were honest with me even when it hurt. They listened, supported, and encouraged me. When I fell, they helped me up and walked with me. When I succeeded, they rejoiced with me. When it was time to stand on my own, they backed off. They allowed me into their lives; I really wasn't alone. Eventually

I was able to give as much as I had received.

It hasn't been quick, easy, or painless, but, by talking, reading, and accepting help from my Higher Power and from EA, I am on my way to recovery one day at a time. I truly believe that if not for the open door of EA, I would still be in the "gray mass of fog," if not already dead or insane.

RECOVERING FROM FEAR

Arlene

About ten years ago, as I was about to say hello to a friend at a large department store, a wave of fear came over me. My heart began to pound, my legs felt like rubber, I started to feel light-headed. I had to get out of the store. I turned and ran. By the time I returned to the car my fear started subsiding. I sat behind the steering wheel, hands still trembling, trying to clear my mind and make some sense out of what was happening to me.

It wasn't the first time I had experienced such fear, but it was the worst. And, because I had run out on my friend in the store, I now added a new emotion to my list—shame. I was ashamed that I had acted as I had. How could I tell my friend the reason I had left the store so quickly was that I was experiencing fear?

So began my life of seclusion and lies.

I began to stay at home more and more, afraid another panic attack would hit me and I would have to flee. I don't know what was worse, the fear of actually going through the panic, or the embarrassment that would come should someone find out about my runaway emotions. I became afraid of both the panic and the fear of being exposed.

So I began to give more and more excuses and lies as to why I couldn't or wouldn't go out to social events. What if another panic attack would occur? How would I get away? What if I embarrassed myself? What would my friends or family think of me? I was an adult. Only small children are afraid. Every time I thought about leaving the house I said, "What if?"

Consequently I spent more and more time at home alone, avoiding the people and places that I felt would bring on another attack. I was so ashamed of how I felt, and what was happening to me. I felt no one would understand, or worse that they would think I was acting like a child, instead of a responsible, rational adult. Too ashamed to even go to a doctor, I kept my irrational fears to myself. Soon my only friends were those who I would talk to on the telephone.

During a television program I learned about Emotions Anonymous. I wanted more out of life, or should I say I wanted to start living life. I had heard of Alcoholics Anonymous, but Emotions Anonymous was something I was not familiar with. I didn't know anything about the Twelve Steps or how the meetings were run. I did know that I needed help.

I found a meeting near my house and with much fear and trepidation I attended my first meeting. I came in late and sat very near the door so I could leave quickly if I had to. It was a step meeting and they were discussing Step Four. For the life of me I could not understand what they were talking about, what the steps were, or even why I was there. As the meeting continued I heard people speak about where they are now in the EA program and where they were when they came into EA. I was amazed to find that there were adults there who had experienced the same fears I had and, with the help of EA and the steps, had turned their lives around. Had I not been at such a low point in my life I doubt if I would have gone. However, I knew that it was time to turn my life around. And, after attending that first meeting, I somehow knew Emotions Anonymous could do that for me.

It wasn't easy, and it wasn't fast. At first I came to the meetings just to hear other people talk about their out-of-control emotions. I sat in the back, talked to no one and was the first to leave. But I kept coming back, congratulating myself that I had even left the house that day. I heard stories, some ringing with positive words of having overcome an emotional hurdle, others talking about the difficulties they were experiencing that week, and yes, even those that were in total despair. But the overall feeling I had on leaving the meeting was that if so many had experienced recovery, people like myself, people who were neither less nor more intelligent than I, then so could I. And I came back. Meeting after meeting I came back.

After many meetings it began to sink in, and I now felt I was beginning to work the steps. I read the book, read the meditations in the EA Today book, worked the steps, and finally, for the first time, took my turn at speaking at the meeting. "Hello, my name is Arlene and I am powerless over my fears." No one laughed, no one made me feel ashamed. My voice quivered, there were tears in my eyes, and I doubt if I made sense to anyone, but I had spoken for the first time at a meeting and a weight had been lifted from me.

Those at that meeting understood. Those at that meeting reached out to me. Those at that meeting gave me words of encouragement. Those at that meeting became my friends — my good, non-judgmental, caring friends.

However, attending meetings, working the Twelve Steps, reading the literature, I knew was not enough. I had to begin putting into practice all I had learned at the meetings. I very hesitantly volunteered to be in charge of the refreshment table. That was easy, all I had to do was make sure the coffee pot was on and there was a supply of cups. Soon I felt comfortable and at ease. I then began to greet newcomers. This proved to be a little more difficult. When I felt comfortable doing this, I then volunteered to be group secretary. This I consider to be my greatest achievement.

My duties were to open the meeting room, begin and end the meeting and wait until all the members were gone in order to lock up. Remember, I was the one who used to come late, sit by the door and leave before the end of the meeting because of my fears. For the first time in years I had made a commitment, and I knew others were depending on me. I called upon everything I had learned at those EA meetings. I placed my trust in my Higher Power as well as in those attending the meeting. When I heard myself saying I had to be perfect, I told myself that I only had to be perfectly human. I let go and turned my fears and anxieties over to my Higher Power.

I was group secretary for the entire Twelve Steps, never missing a meeting, never entering late. Many of the members came up to me after the meeting and told me how well I had done. They said I had done a good job. I felt great! Many knew how far I had come in my recovery and rejoiced with me.

I could tell you that all of my fears are gone, but I would be lying. The truth is I am active in my community, I am no longer afraid to go out and meet people, and I have started enjoying life. I am living my life one day at a time, and, with the help of Emotions Anonymous, I will continue to grow and be who and what I was created to be.

If I can reach out to just one person with my story, then I feel I will have accomplished something. I must tell you that it won't be easy, nothing worthwhile ever is. You may find yourself giving all kinds of excuses as to why you should not go to a meeting. I know that I did. You may say you will never understand the steps, but you will. You may tell yourself that you have nothing in common with the people who attend an EA meeting, but look again. Isn't that your story she is telling? And isn't that the same feeling you felt that the gentleman at the end of the table is talking about? Love and support, understanding and healing are present at Emotions Anonymous meetings. Stick around long enough to experience it. I did, and it changed my entire life.

My Life Will Be Great When ...

Barb

When I came into the program over twenty-four years ago, I had been suffering severe depression for two years. During that time I was so unhappy with who I was that I came very close to suicide twice. I was married and had two lovely children, so I had many of the things that are supposed to make us happy in life. But I didn't like myself or my life, and I came very close to ending it.

One of the most significant areas of my past was my attitude toward being a woman. I had the idea that every little girl grew up to be a wife and mother. There were few other acceptable things to be. I wanted to be the perfect woman, have the perfect house, and the perfect husband and children. Obviously, I wasn't going to find *perfect* anything, so I was very disappointed.

I married my high school sweetheart when I was eighteen. He wasn't sophisticated enough for me (he was a farmer), but I decided I would change him to suit me. We had identical twin girls nine months after we were married.

As a perfect woman I knew that to be successful I had to make my husband successful. In those days everyone who had a degree was successful. I did get him to quit his job and attend college. It was tough in student housing with two small children, but I was building for the future. Today didn't matter much.

I lost a lot of weight after the babies were born, and, when I began to gain a little back, my doctor put me on something wonderful — amphetamines. I had so much energy for work, at home, and attending school. When I quit taking them I crashed. My doctor didn't know what had happened, and that was the beginning of the downward spiral. Much more was involved, including a kidney infection, but the bottom line was there were many things I never acknowledged or dealt with.

I discovered I had always had a low self-image and was basically a shy person even though I put on the show that I was an extrovert. I always told myself a woman had to be ten times better than a man to be equal. The real fact of the matter was I had to be ten times better than anyone else to feel equal. This goes back to my feelings of inadequacy.

I tried a professional, pills, a pastor, a marriage counselor, and couldn't find any of the answers. I expected the answers to be handed to me on a silver platter, but the answers had to come from within me. With those expectations, a professional could not help me.

I attended an EA meeting a few times and backed away from it. There were too many steps that mentioned God. I didn't think that would work. Then, as each possible solution failed, I eventually came back to the program. I also accepted the fact that the answers had to come from within me.

Adopting our interracial baby should have made me feel much better because we had put him off for so long. While the baby brought much happiness into our lives, I had to deal with what was within me.

My husband had started this program when we first found it, and he remained there. I eventually came back because I saw him changing. He stopped playing the sick games we had always played, and he was feeling better about himself. He had a lot of friends who cared about him. This seemed like hope to me. I went to a different meeting than he for at least three years. I often joke that when we first started the program he was a real jerk. He has turned into the neatest person (maybe he always was), and he is now my best friend. I never thought that would have been possible before the program.

I searched for a Higher Power. My concept was hell, fire, and brimstone which wasn't conducive to working this program. I heard people in my group talking about their Higher Power. Although I didn't know exactly what they had, I wanted the feelings they described.

I searched for months and found a real God, one who is loving and forgiving. It was totally different from the God of my childhood. It has been one of the best things that happened to me through this program. I know that each of us finds God in our own way.

The program taught me that if a degree is important to me, then I needed to have that as a goal for me — not for my husband. I returned to school part-time, worked full-time, and took care of three children and a house. I didn't maneuver that on my own. It was obviously God's will for me.

During the years my husband and I were raising our three children, there were wonderful times with them, and times that were not so wonderful. We ended up dealing with dependency issues with two of our children. It was very painful, but I learned a lot and became closer to them by working through the situations. I've had the privilege of watching all three of them grow up to be very special, wonderful adults. They are my friends, and I know they are always there for me. Our family has become more healthy through dealing with the problems.

My career grew by leaps and bounds after I received my degree. Within a few years I was asked to transfer to Seattle, Washington. My husband was delighted. This was really positive for my self-esteem. A few years later I was again asked to transfer, this time to Ft. Worth, Texas to help start a new venture. A few years later I went to yet another subsidiary, still in Ft. Worth. I was then able to work less overtime and devote some time to myself. I completed the CPA exam and lost 117 pounds after battling a lifetime with weight problems. I had completed all of the goals I had ever set for myself, and I felt good about myself — or so I thought.

Then in late 1992, I experienced another round of deep depression. I didn't believe that after all these years I could again return to those depths. I would have told you I had dealt with all my issues prior to this time, but I discovered my mind had not let me see yet what all the issues were.

I don't completely know why it happened then, but my mother had a heart attack, and I went home to spend time with my family. It was so enjoyable. I guess my mind finally told me it was safe to work on the issues I had tucked away. I also had surgery earlier that year. Everything was fine until I accidentally took the pain medication thinking it was my potassium, and it threw me into a tailspin that I couldn't stop by myself. Within a short time I was suicidal again. I experienced severe pain that I didn't know was still possible. It was very frightening to go through this again.

When I experienced my first major depression twenty-six years ago, I tried professionals and pills, and they didn't work. This time I discovered what advances had been made in the field, and what competent professionals in my life can mean. I remember twenty-six years ago asking if what I was going through could be a heredity condition. They said no, it was just a trauma I was going through. Today the first thing the professionals said was that they thought I had a chemical imbalance because of my family history. My father had a nervous breakdown when I was born, his mother had died in a mental hospital, and his sister had also gone through a breakdown. I discovered what medication can mean to me. It can help me feel like a normal person. I will be on medication as long as my doctor thinks it is necessary. It is like blood pressure medication. If my body needs it, I will take it.

During this episode of depression I kept sinking, and eventually we decided that a partial hospitalization was indicated. I couldn't go inpatient because of the images of my father being carried off and locked up. That was too frightening to imagine. The partial hospitalization was every evening of the week for a couple of months. This was one of the best things I've done for myself because it was a concentration of working on the things that my mind was slowly letting me remember. I thought I knew all about myself after working my fourth and fifth steps, and all the years in the program. I knew only what my mind would let me know. Now I needed to get rid of the tormenting images that I had locked up.

There were many childhood issues that I didn't know were there. There are memories I still can't access, only bits and pieces. The therapists I dealt with seemed pretty sure of the nature of this trauma, and I dealt with it as if. It's not important if I ever get the memories back. I have dealt with the general nature of the abuse.

I also discovered I have an eating disorder. Whenever I heard this term in the past I would recoil, for certainly I didn't have that. When I sought help I had many symptoms of anorexia, and I am bulimic. I'm not anorexic anymore. Through my healing I have gained some of my weight back, and I feel confident that when I am fully healed, and my thyroid condition is under control, my body will let the weight come off.

I have had many physical problems in the past few years, such as diabetes, ulcerated esophagus (which may not have been caused by the bulimia), and, most recently, hypothyroidism. But, having worked through some of the issues in my life has helped me to become healthier.

EA is a wonderful support program. It doesn't replace the professionals in my life when I need them. I'm sure this is why so many professionals refer people to EA — to have support and to learn how to live a new way of life.

I know that my mind is like a computer, constantly recording events that happen. When it is safe for my mind to deal with the issues, it will allow me to see them. It is very uncomfortable at times, and someday I may know myself entirely.

I am very thankful to God for my husband, children, and new grandbaby, as well as parents and sister and brothers. I am also very grateful for EA, that I found it when I did, for it has kept me alive all of these years as I've dealt with a chemical imbalance I didn't know I had. I know that life is a gift, and to keep the gift I need to be working on myself.

A LIFE OF ANGER

Al

Life has been extremely hard for me, but I do not want people to feel sorry for me. At one time I couldn't talk about my past because my emotions would get to me, and I would just break down and have to go into another room and be by myself. I find it easier now to talk about it.

I begin my story at about eight years of age. Around this age my father decided I was big enough to work, and he pulled me out of school. He had his own business building concrete foundations under houses. The wood forms were about eight feet high and perhaps ten to twelve inches wide. It was my job to get inside the forms and remove the spacing blocks. There wasn't much crawl space. I was always afraid the workers would forget about me in the forms and pour the concrete in on top of me. The longer I worked, the more angry I became, for I knew I should be in school. However, I was too afraid of my father to say anything. This continued for the next three years when my parents went their separate ways, and I found myself in a farm foster home.

For the next three years I was moved from farm to farm, and I was forced to work at chores beginning at 6:00 a.m. I never went back to school, and I missed it. There was nothing I could do about it. It seemed that every time I began to feel a part of the family I was living with I was moved to the next foster family. I suppose they ran out of foster homes, for I was finally sent to Toronto and placed in a training school.

There I had six years of pure hell, being abused in every way possible. I thought this was the way people were supposed to be. I was angry and furious. I would go out to the track and put ten pounds of lead weights on my feet to run around the track to get the anger out of me. I would do this for hours. If I had dropped dead, I wouldn't have given a damn because I wanted to get out of this world.

When I left there at age twenty, I went back home to my father. I figured I would give him a second chance. I went to work for him again, this time in the bush cutting cord wood. Things weren't too bad at first, but he got the money and I got nothing. After a short stay in the hospital, I gave him the bill. He said, "It's your bill. You pay it." We argued, and, although he was not paying me for my work, he wasn't going to pay this bill. I was furious. I took his car one night to get away for a while. He knew I had it, but he had me charged with car theft. I went to jail and did time for this.

While in jail, I thought about suicide, for I didn't really want to stay in this world. I came close quite a few times. When I got out of jail, I had two things in my life — anger and hatred for every man in the world. I had nowhere to go so I returned to my father, but it didn't work out.

I left home and roamed the streets not knowing what to do with my life and being fearful of every man I saw. The only things I had to eat at that time were frozen apple cores and banana and orange peels. I was too afraid to steal although I was very hungry most of the time. I kept this up for two or three years — working here, working there, whatever job I could get. I survived out of fear — afraid my father would find me, afraid of the law, and afraid of survival.

Finally when I got enough nerve to work with somebody, I got a job driving a tractor trailer across the country. I figured now I could deal with my anger, but, no, it was always near the surface. I had a lot of good friends in the trucking business, but all we had in common was booze or dope. This helped me for a while. I took dope to keep awake for seven days at a time. I took pills to stay awake and took pills to put me to sleep. I wish I had all the money I spent on booze and drugs during that time. I once bought a forty-ounce bottle in Calgary and had it finished by the time I reached Winnipeg. If I had been stopped by the police I would not have been able to stand up. That's the kind of life I led then; it was tough.

There were times my anger got to me so bad, the hatred, everything I had in me. I sometimes would be driving on the steep grades through the mountains, and I would stand on the running board at sixty or seventy miles per hour trying to find the courage to jump. What stopped me was the thought, "What would happen if I jumped off the truck and the truck hit another car." I couldn't take somebody else with me.

I finally decided to stop the heavy drinking and stick to the pills. There were many times I had to stop on the side of the road because my nerves were shaking so bad. I would sit on the ground until the trembling and shaking stopped, sometimes as long as ten or fifteen minutes. When it was over, I would kick the hell out of the tires to vent my anger and frustration. I knew the tires were the one thing I could pound on and not have to worry about retaliation.

I met a woman and my life settled for a short time, but it was not to last. Due to my own stupidity I ended up in a minimum security prison farm, and I was back on the pills. I was taking six pills to calm my nerves and another four to put me to sleep. I seemed to be okay as long as I used these pills, but the old thoughts of suicide returned. It was a daily struggle to survive.

I found EA in that prison. I met a guy in prison, and he asked me to come to the EA meeting. For over a month he badgered me until I finally said yes. I listened for a while, but left convinced this was not for me. I didn't need this.

About three months later I ended up in the psych ward where neither they nor I knew what to do with me. We all knew that if I was left alone too long I'd be six feet under the ground. My friend was able to visit, and he said to me, "Why don't you wake up. Yeah, quit being like a stone. You're rolling all the time. You got that hatred in you and can't do nothing." I had seen many psychiatrists, but the only results were "come back next week."

When I was finally released from the ward my friend suggested EA again. I decided to give it another shot. An EA volunteer was at the meeting. We were able to talk for about two hours. I felt such a relief in being able to talk to her openly, and she actually had some answers for me. It was wonderful to talk to her, and I started going to the meetings regularly after that. The meetings in prison are a bit different from those in the community. The members in prison get down to the core problems more quickly in the two-hour meetings. You're dealing with all kinds of offenders, some even murderers, and when they talk they mean it.

After about a month I told my psychiatrist to keep his pills, but he kept prescribing them. When I had finally saved about a cup full (they were prescribed one at a time), I gave them to the desk officer telling him I didn't need them any more. He congratulated me and suggested I may soon be ready for parole.

In EA I had found people who took an interest in me, believed what I was saying, and were willing to listen. I found somebody who had been through it before, somebody who understood. I had found a caring family that I never had in childhood. The child within began to appear. At age fifty-two I was finally able to cry and allow that child to express his fears and hatred to another person after stuffing and hiding my feelings for so many years. Now that I am out of prison, I see a psychologist every week, and I attend my weekly EA meeting. At one time I went to three or four meetings a week, but now I am down to my one regular weekly meeting. My anger is not there like it used to be. It can be more or less controlled now. I can accept hugs from the female members, but am still leery about the men. This too is improving, and my trust is slowly being renewed. Since really getting involved with my EA group, committing suicide is out of the question. I would miss my EA family, the people I can talk to. The nightmares, when I dreamed of suicide and woke up drenched with perspiration, are gone completely.

I am no longer so quick to anger. I can allow others to have their own opinions. I have learned to say no to others when I don't want to do something. I now can look after myself first and others second. Before it was reversed.

I need this fellowship. I need my EA family. I need the meetings. I see everybody at meetings, and I can say to myself, "You aren't the only one who's got a problem." I thought all my life I was the one that had the problems. But nobody is perfect. What happened to me will never change, but the only way I thought I could block out the memories was to take a gun and shoot myself. I don't have any reason to do that anymore. I don't have those fears. I don't have that anger which was the biggest thing. Anger is one of the many effects life has had on me. It's one of my emotions. I'm going to feel it when it comes my way or else repress it as I have done for years. I've repressed it, but it still wouldn't go away. Now because I am working a good program I can handle it.

I come here to do this for myself. Coming to EA I have learned I can shamelessly feel all my feelings and still take responsibility for what I do. I don't have to let my feelings control me. Now I am being grateful and positive by coming to EA. I never had control of my emotions, but now I am learning to take care of myself emotionally. I know grown men aren't supposed to cry, they are supposed to hide it, but I can't anymore. I talk to people about my life when it is appropriate and safe. I reach out for help now; before, I had too much pride to do that.

I need the hugs that tell me I'm accepted — at last. When I get an EA hug it means something, "Hi friend, how are you? How you doing, how's your week?" EA is not something that I'm forced to go to. The choice is mine. EA is something that I need. I adore it. I enjoy it. EA is part of my life and will be until I'm six feet underground.

Living Inside My Skin

Linda

As far back as I can remember, I have never felt comfortable "living in my skin." I grew up with a lot of trauma and crisis in my family. This included house fires, sexual abuse, family breakdown, as well as my mother's emotional breakdown for which she was hospitalized. She never was to return to the family although she did eventually leave the institution. I used food as my comfort against the loneliness of not having my mom around to comfort me, and I began to put on weight.

Within a few years Dad got involved with a woman who had four children, and they all moved in with us. The crisis and chaos continued to get progressively worse. We became a blended family which never blended. During that time I was sexually molested for the second time, and I couldn't tell anyone.

We didn't get spankings in our house — we got beatings with belt buckles, kettle cords, wooden spoons, anything my step-mother could get her hands on. I became a people pleaser to avoid her wrath, but nothing seemed to work to make her happy and eventually I got another beating.

I grew up in an era where the parents were the authority. Their word was law, and they never made mistakes. I was taught never to question authority. I was told I shouldn't feel that way, and if I didn't quit crying I'd be given something to cry about.

Being the oldest girl, by the time I was nine years old I was responsible for the housework, laundry, ironing, cooking, and disciplining of the children (not an easy feat when my brother was older and my step-brother was stronger than me).

We lived two different lifestyles. When dad was away fishing, which he did for a living, we lived like gypsies — walking around barefoot, eating and sleeping and traveling when we felt like it. When dad was home we had to live like a "normal" family with three meals a day, eating at a table at a set time every day.

There was a lot of favoritism and taking sides in our family. The family resorted to low-blows and character assassination techniques such as: "you're stupid," "you're dumb," "you're fat and ugly." There were mixed messages like "you're so stupid" and "you should know better than that" being said in the same breath. The very lowest of low-blows was "you're as crazy as your mother."

With all the confusion, chaos, and dysfunction going on in and around me, I felt crazy, but I denied it because I so wanted to be normal and to *fit in*. I would go to any lengths to fit in.

During my early teen years things got progressively worse. I was depressed and suicidal. In order to stop or deny "the crazies" I began drinking. I wanted to drink to be cool, to be accepted, and to forget my problems, but I got caught. I got beaten and grounded, and then I would do it again. I felt fat, ugly, unloved, and unlovable. I hated living at home, but didn't know how to leave.

I eventually did leave home. I quit school and attached myself to the first man who would take me. Needless to say, that didn't work. I began to live a life of self-will run riot. I figured, "I'm an adult now and no one is gonna tell me what to do!" I smoked and drank and picked up men. I worked sometimes and lived on the welfare system most of the time.

For the next seventeen years I lived in a downward spiral — a self-made hell. I kept looking for love in all the wrong places. People would tell me that no one could love me until I loved myself. My self-pity response to that was, "How could I learn to love myself when even my family didn't love me? You know a child learns what they live." Everyone told me that no one could do it for me; I had to do it myself. I didn't want to! I didn't know how! My life was hell, and I felt crazy, but I tried to deny it. I felt lonely, unloved, and unlovable, but I tried so desperately hard to please others so they would love me. I felt I was a sinner and would burn in hell. I didn't know how to change nor did I have the willingness to do anything about it. It was easier to place my power in the hands of others. If things didn't work out, I could always blame them.

I had always felt the "When I get. . . I'll be happy" syndrome. I kept feeling one day my knight in shining armor would rescue me from my life of pain, fear, and loneliness. All I had ever wanted in life was someone to love me unconditionally, take care of me, and protect me from the big, bad world. That's quite a burden to lay on another human being!

I was a binge drinker. I could go several months without a drink, but once I started drinking I couldn't stop until all the booze or all the money ran out. It seemed that I could hold all my emotions in for so long and then I would either explode or have to drown them through the bottle. I would either be a very passive, depressed person, or I would be a vocal rage-aholic. It took another six months in a downwards spiral to hell before I became willing to surrender and admit absolute defeat.

I found myself more and more out of control. My drinking picked up, and it took me places I did not want to go. I found myself having affairs with married men. I knew my years of sexual abuse had finally caught up with me, and I had to do something about it because it was affecting all my relationships. But I didn't know how to change it or how to get help. There was a lot of fear stopping me. I was afraid no one would believe me or that they would say I brought it on myself just as my family had said.

It came to the point where I had to admit my life was unmanageable, and I could not do it alone. My first call was to a sexual assault hot line. I was heard and understood, but I couldn't get in to see a counselor for two weeks. I knew I couldn't hold the pain inside for another two weeks. I had to do something *now*. So I looked for the ad for EA I had seen previously in our local paper, and I got myself to the next meeting.

I didn't know anything about twelve-step programs, how to

conduct myself in the meetings, or how much or how little to share, but I knew I qualified – I had known that for a long time. When they asked me to share at that first meeting, I verbally puked my life story on the table for all to see. I let out some of the pain, guilt, and shame. The people were patient and understanding with me. They patted my back and handed me some Kleenex and told me to "Keep coming back – it works." Well, I didn't know what "It" was that worked, but it sure felt good in those rooms. I wanted more so I kept coming back. It felt like I had finally come home.

I had a hard time with the "God shit" in the beginning, but I knew the people in those rooms were getting better and better. I wanted what they had. I felt better after a meeting so I kept coming back. I didn't have much belief and faith in the God I grew up with. That God was one of all power and punishment. Growing up I had been told every time I walked into a church that I was a sinner and I would burn in hell, so I lived my life accordingly. I figured if I was going to go to hell, I may as well make it worth the trip.

Eventually I heard *God, as you understand Him,* and that helped me to settle down and start working the program. The only thing I could understand in the beginning was that the meetings and the people in the meetings helped me calm down inside my skin for a few hours at a time. In the beginning I used the group meetings as a power greater than myself; like they say, there's strength in numbers. I really wanted to get this program *right,* but I didn't know how to find a God of my understanding. So I looked toward nature initially for an all powerful God of my understanding. My concept of God keeps changing as I keep changing. Sometimes God is what I call the "God-spark" inside all of us, sometimes it's the universe, sometimes it's love, sometimes it's my morals, and in reality it's probably a combination of all of the above.

Because I had hurt so bad for so long, I wanted to "get well yesterday." I had to find a way to get well fast. I knew all the meetings in the world, all the talks over coffee, and all the readings weren't going to make me well. I had to do the work. I believed it was only by working the steps that it was going to make a difference inside me. I made a commitment to myself to write out all the steps following the Step by Step guide. It was very hard and very emotional, but I learned a lot and let go of a lot.

I saw that my biggest dis-ease is denial. I did not want to accept reality, myself, people, places, or things exactly as they were. I wanted to change everything to suit me and my self-centered ways. When I first came to EA the two phrases that I hated the most were that I was self-centered and insane. I denied I was self-centered because I was such a people-pleaser and martyr. How could I possibly be self-centered when I was always doing for others? Today I see I always had a hidden agenda in doing for others — namely that they would like me, accept me, and love me. And as far as insanity? Well, I had always felt crazy. Now the older I get and the more recovery I get, the less normal I want to be. I want to be the unique creation God wants me to be. For me, today, insanity is being something other than myself in order for you to accept me and love me.

All my life I could never figure out what life was all about. All I could see was that I was put here to die, and life sucked. I experienced a lot of hurt and loss and pain in a short period of time, and I couldn't see it letting up. What I realize now is that I lived a life of blame, irresponsibility, and self-centeredness. Today I have hope for a better life through this new way of life. Today I have a purpose in life — to love myself and others, to help others, and to do God's will. I believe God's will is to just be the best *me* I can be 'cuz he only made one of me.

This program has shown me that I am okay. I am loved and loveable. I am worthy and worthwhile. The EA people showed me, for the first time in my life, unconditional love and acceptance. Not everybody liked me when I came around nor does everybody like me today, but they provided an air of seeming acceptance. And that was enough for me.

I still make mistakes, less major and less often. Sometimes I am still judgmental and intolerant of others, but not for as long when I remember where I was and what I was like when I first came to EA. I still get angry with myself and others, but I can look at the unrealistic expectation I have and let it go more easily. This is a program of progress rather than perfection, and I thank God for that! When I slip I remind myself that recovery is a process, not a destination.

The program really does help me to live with unsolved problems. I use the Serenity Prayer to figure out what to do with a problem. I can either accept it or change it, and I ask God for the courage and power to carry that out. I use the slogans to help me through a crisis and remind myself that "This too shall pass." My favorite slogan is "Know yourself — be honest," ever reminding myself that I have a dis-ease of denial and only rigorous self-honesty will help me arrest this dis-ease. Today there are so many tools at my disposal to help me with my everyday living, if I but pick them up and use them. The choice is mine!

The promises are coming true for me, especially "No matter how far down the scale we have gone, we can see how our experiences can benefit others," and "We do not regret the past or wish to shut the door on it." I am comforted by the thought at the end of the promises which says recovery happens "sometimes quickly, sometimes slowly."

When I walked through the doors of EA nearly five years ago, I was in a major clinical depression. I was drinking uncontrollably, and I was sexually promiscuous. I had low self-esteem, and I was filled with guilt, shame, rage, resentments, and what I term "black toxic ooze."

After about nine months in EA, I made a conscious decision to maintain sobriety in order to honestly practice EA and to feel my emotions rather than drown them. I've been sober for four years. Today I try to practice celibacy until the day I find that special someone. My self-esteem is greatly improved, although I still have my down days. For the most part the guilt and shame and black toxic ooze have dissipated, although occasionally I still hit some pockets stemming from unresolved issues from the past. Today I can live, for the most part, comfortably inside my skin.

One of the most rewarding parts of my recovery is carrying the message. I am asked to sponsor people and help them work the steps. I am asked to be a speaker to inmates and at conventions. I was asked by a fellow EA member to submit my story for this publication. I don't think these things would be possible if I didn't work this program, work the steps, and have some recovery to share with others.

What helped me? EA. The people in EA. The EA big book. The EA *Today* book and other literature, including the *Message* magazine. A willingness to be honest, open-minded, and willing to diligently work this program to the best of my ability. Most importantly, I found a loving God of my understanding, and I maintain conscious contact through prayer and meditation.

Like I tell the inmates I speak to, if just one person finds help and hope by my sharing my story, my life will not have been a waste. May God bless you in your journey through recovery.

IT WAS A DARK AND STORMY NIGHT

Ken

My name is Ken, and I am powerless over my emotions. I used to think I was vulnerable to most of my emotions, but certainly not powerless. I am sure this misconception only made my problems worse.

I was raised in a small town in southern Minnesota. I am the oldest of four children from a typical Scandinavian family. We were not an expressive group. As children we were taught to keep our emotions under control. The old sayings, "big boys don't cry" and "children should be seen and not heard" were our way of life. We were taught to stuff our feelings, especially our anger. Don't let anything show. My mother was a "fixer," always trying to keep the peace at any cost rather than let the emotion of the minute run its course and try to deal and learn from it. I think that this stuffing allowed for an emotional build-up that was released in totally inappropriate ways when something occurred to set it off.

We were taught that perfection was expected. There was rarely an encouraging word when something was done well, but a lot of condemnation when something was done wrong. I learned to beat myself up pretty well when I didn't perform to the very best even when I knew I had given my best effort. Perfectionism and low self-esteem can be a very deadly combination.

After I finished high school, I went to a small church college. Here we lived in a strict environment where the lessons I learned at home were reinforced. It didn't help that I studied a rigid, precise curriculum either. Following school was work, marriage, and a family. The pressures that came with these were even tougher to handle. I was totally unprepared.

I was introduced to EA at a time when what I believed to be important elements of my life were being systematically stripped away. My family was breaking up, I was losing my home, my economic security was in jeopardy, my job was miserable, and what was left of my self-esteem was being totally destroyed. Maybe I could have handled these things one at a time, but when they came all at once, the load was just too great. I was a mess.

At this time I was working with a man who had been in EA for many years. One day he walked into my office and dropped the EA book on my desk with just a few words, "Maybe something in here will help you." There were no explanations, no shoulds, just a maybe. Being in an agitated state of mind, it took me a few weeks before I even started to read the book. When I finally did, I was ready to grab on to anything that would give me some serenity. My journey in EA began.

Things that I read struck a receptive chord, and I made the decision to go to a meeting. I called the EA Service Center and was told where meetings were being held. Even then, I had several second thoughts; thirds and fourths, even. When the day finally came, I got in the car leaving early to be sure I could find the meeting place in time. I almost backed out several times on the way. Every intersection was another opportunity to quit. My expectations were that this would be a group of women discussing their *feelings,* and I would be totally out of place being a male. Besides they would probably be talking about something I knew nothing about. I went anyway, and I am so very glad I did.

The first person I met was exactly the person I needed at that time. She welcomed me and did her best to make me feel comfortable when that was the last thing I was feeling. The first meeting for me was on Step Eight—not a good beginning. I had hurt so many people and making a list of them would be a difficult task. I wasn't sure I would come back again if it was all going to be that tough. However, I did learn something very important that first night – I was not alone. I was surprised when the meeting was over and several people came over and offered hugs. It was the first time in over two years that I had had a hug, even from my own kids.

The first few weeks were difficult, but I kept going. After a month or so, I started going to a second meeting—the same one my mentor went to. It was a good move as I was able to get a wide range of perspectives from the people at the two groups. My regular group was composed of people who had been involved in the program for five or six years where the econd group had people who had been active fifteen years or more. I was doubly blessed.

Gradually the program started to take hold. I started to think, to feel, and to evaluate how and what I was feeling. This was new behavior for me. I struggled to do some of the steps and when I couldn't do them according to the standards I had set for myself, my old tapes started to play in my mind. "I'm not good enough; I can't do anything right." Fortunately, Harold held my hand through the tough times and kept me from quitting.

I had the hardest time with Step Four, the inventory. My education had taught me to analyze everything in detail, and this was how I approached the step. I caused myself much unnecessary pain. I had reached the point where I had to do a Step Five even if it wasn't perfect in order to move ahead. I approached that meeting with much trepidation nonetheless. Here I was going to tell another person how bad a person I really was, and he was going to agree with me. I wasn't sure I would be able to handle the censure. I was wrong. It wasn't nearly as intimidating as I had expected. My inventory wasn't perfect, and *that was all right!* It surprised me that I realized that.

I have often said to my groups that the greatest benefit I have received from the program is a sense of awareness. I can see how my thoughts can lead to a feeling — good or bad — that can impact how I relate to those around me. I can see in advance how something I might do or say can give me discomfort. I am able to experience my emotions as they occur. In the past if I felt a need to cry, I would question why and try to stop. Now, I don't fight it, I just let it flow, and I am better for it.

The second benefit I have received is acceptance. I can accept others and myself. I still have the need to do things perfectly, but if I try my best I can accept it if I'm not perfect. This is freeing. I cannot remember the last time I put myself down or got angry with someone else. I never thought I would be able to say that.

EA has given me tools to live with. The slogans are my constant companions. I refer to them as my mental choke chains, reminding me to think. The *Just for Todays* are my help when things get rough. The EA people are my second family, and they accept me.

My story has no ending. I am a becoming. I can find so many ways to grow in the EA program. I continue to go to meetings, to the one day retreats, the weekend retreats, and the conventions when I am able. It is a rich experience. Above all, I try to work the program the best I can. I'll try to get it right, but if I don't, that's okay. My Higher Power guides me, and my EA friends support me.

FILLING THE HOLE IN MY HEART

Miriam

Shalom! My name is Miriam, and I am powerless over my emotions. I am writing to share with you the good news of recovery – the recovery I have experienced through the Twelve Steps of EA.

I am an EA Loner because I am a cloistered nun living in a monastery in the Holy Land. I was introduced to the program by a priest who has had years of experience working the Twelve Steps. At the beginning of a community retreat, I poured out my hurt and pain to him, and, after some careful, prayerful reflection, he replied, "Have you ever heard about the Twelve Steps? I think they could help you to find serenity and peace."

The Twelve Steps? Gosh, well... uh... er... I had attended a couple of twelve-step meetings in the USA almost ten years ago, but it just didn't seem like the right program for me. But today, well.... Then I remembered that in a box of used books we had received, someone had sent us a book called *Emotions Anonymous*. I told Father that I would find it and begin reading. After all, I figured I had nothing to lose, and I was hurting so badly inside that I knew if I didn't get help soon, I would be sent away from the monastery I loved so much.

Reading the introduction, the endorsements, and "The Doctor's Opinion" at the beginning of the book was a little like testing the water temperature at the end of a swimming pool. I wanted help, but I was hesitant; nonetheless, I kept reading. By the time I reached the chapter, "Enormity of Emotional Illness," I was ready to take the big plunge. Everything I read described my life and my illness with penetrating accuracy.

I returned to talk with our retreat master, and I shared with Father some of the insights and awareness that I had gained in my reading. I told him that I wanted to try working the Twelve Steps, and he promised to help me. During the entire week I meditated on what I read, and I shared my insights, my thoughts and feelings with Father. By the end of the retreat, I had made the first three steps, and I was committed to continue even after Father left. Thank God, he promised to stay in touch!

If my beginnings in EA seem unusual to you, I want you to know that the beginnings of my emotional illness are very, very ordinary. Reading your stories helped to unlock closets full of dark memories for me as I worked Step Four, my inventory. I would like to share some of my story, too, hoping that it can help someone else who's starting the EA program.

I am an American, a Hoosier in the Holy Land. I grew up surrounded by cornfields in rural Indiana, the first of two daughters born to an ordinary, hard-working, 1950's-era family. Dad was a carpenter and Mom was a homemaker, and for nearly five years I was an only child. My parents wanted to raise a *happy* little Hoosier, and they made specific choices to reinforce that emotion.

Whenever I was angry, I was given something to eat, and I soon learned to go by myself to the bread drawer to deal with my anger. So, I became a fat little Hoosier. I've discovered through working the Twelve Steps that I am also powerless over food.

Fear was not acceptable either, and my childhood was full of fear. I was in terror of going to bed alone at night, so I had to sleep with a light on, clutching something soft and warm, and sucking my thumb — all of which continued until I was around seven years old. I also was a chronic bed-wetter, and I grew to feel very guilty for feeling afraid. Eventually I bypassed the feeling of fear and went straight to guilt feelings.

Sadness and tears were also off-limits because "big girls don't cry." Yet, the older I grew, the sadder and more depressed I became. The television was closely supervised, and we only watched television as a family activity. Cartoons, game shows, variety shows, and comedies were the only programs permitted; no dramas or mysteries were seen on our TV. Laughter was the only appropriate emotional response.

Underneath all of my mixed-up emotions was a big, gaping hole in my hollow, broken heart. In our little family there was very little physical or verbal affection. I always assumed that it was normal. No one said, "I love you," because love was something to be done, not spoken. My days alone at home with Mom were solitary days, and I learned to live without hugs and kisses. I was always "daddy's girl," and his arrival in the evening brought some relief, but not enough. My emotional needs were immense, and I had very few options for meeting those needs. It seemed that food and my active imagination were the only resources I had.

I sensed deep down inside that I was on shaky ground when my younger sister was born. Already feeling deprived of love and affection, her arrival only made matters worse. A resentment toward her began to grow, and it grew and remained until my fourth and fifth steps.

The remainder of my childhood and adolescence was marked by my hunger for love and the increasing desire to find ways to meet my emotional needs. Somehow, those needs always remained unmet, and the hole in my heart grew bigger and bigger. That hole became an abyss of sadness and despair; by age sixteen I was one very depressed Hoosier. My father's unexpected death from a heart attack was the ultimate blow. My emotional responses were confused and inappropriate. I refused to cry, I became a "pillar of strength," and I was praised by both family and friends for my behavior. Two years later, I had to be admitted to a psychiatric hospital.

My experiences in therapy helped me get in touch with my feelings. I improved, and I was healthier than ever. I was able to excel in college and graduate school, build a good career, gain respect and material success, but the basic need for love and affection still remained unaddressed and unmet.

I was a slave to that need; I did everything I could to meet it. Money, sex, and power, and, of course, food were my favorite outlets, but the satisfaction was fleeting. I learned eventually just to bandage up that hole in my heart.

Thanks to my Higher Power, the God who is Love gradually attracted me more than anything or anyone else. My conversion was slow, gentle, progressive, and profound. Because of God, I eventually chose to give up money, sex, and power for a life of poverty, chastity, and obedience. For Love alone, I left everything to come to the Holy Land, to live alone with Love.

I found Love in the monastery, but I also found myself because my emotional illness came with me. Despite all the praise and approval of my superiors, I was crazy from unaccepted and inappropriate emotions. It's not easy to live day and night within the same small four walls with other women who don't know about or work the Twelve Steps. Besides, my Superior seemed to be a carbon copy of my mom, and the Sister sitting next to me reminded me exactly of my younger sister back home again in Indiana. There I was, trying so hard to be the ideal nun, all because I wanted to be loved by my Sisters and by God. But deep down inside, I was frozen by fears, eaten alive by anger and resentment, and I was drowning in depression. I never exploded, though; instead of exploding, I was imploding. The harder I tried to control myself and things or people around me, the more out of control I became. Needless to say, despite all the apparent order and control in monastic life, my own life was out of control and very unmanageable.

Today, thanks to God, I have a new and beautiful story to tell. Through months and months of working the Twelve Steps of EA, I have gained a serenity never before imagined. My broken heart is no longer hollow because my heart is filled every day, one day at a time, by Love himself. I rejoice in my brokenness, in my emotional illness, because it is the point where God, my Higher Power, loves me in my poverty and powerlessness.

Today, I thank God for my illness because it is also my living link with you; it is a special bond that cannot be broken. My consecrated life is based on the promise that my daily prayer and all that I suffer is used by God to help you in your needs. I need you just as much as you need me — just as together we need God.

Today, I still encounter problems, and I'm still discovering me, but also I'm still asking God to remove my character defects, and I'm still finding new ways to *let go and let God*. All the promises of EA's ninth step are being realized every day in my life. It seems as if my life is becoming a living Serenity Prayer.

A famous saint, St. Therese of Lisieux once wrote a poem for one of her Sisters in their little monastery in Normandy. Full of love and trust in God, she proclaimed: "I've only got today... I've got nothing but today." Just for today, I am working the Twelve Steps of EA, and I thank my Higher Power, the God who is Love, for giving me this beautiful way of life.

TRYING TO FIND THE REAL ME

John

My name is John, and I'm powerless over my emotions. I came to EA searching for a new way of life. After a series of long depressions, manic-episodes, and psychiatric hospitalizations, I knew I needed to find some guidance and a sense of peace and stability in my life. I needed to ground myself firmly in something that had strong meaning. My illness was ruling my life and the medication wasn't working. I had been given just about every anti-depressant on the market, plus tranquilizers, anti-psychotic pills, mood stabilizers, and I even had electric shock treatments. Nothing would relieve the deep depressions and mood swings which tore my life asunder.

After my last hospitalization I started to lose hope. I could no longer adjust to normal everyday living, and the depression started to hit me hard again. I became extremely frustrated. No matter how hard I tried, I seemed unable to get the help I so desperately needed at the time. It seemed to be a never-ending battle.

I knew I couldn't handle this condition on my own, so I started reaching out to others for support. No matter to whom I spoke, no one really seemed to want to listen. It was as if they didn't want to be bothered or they didn't really care. I felt hurt because most people I approached were close friends and family members. They didn't understand what I was going through because none of them had any personal experience with my situation.

I became even more frustrated until I received a phone call from a very special friend who had helped me through my last hospitalization. She too was a patient. The reason she was so special was because she demonstrated a great deal of compassion toward me, even though

I kept to myself a lot and looked as though I didn't want to be bothered. She seemed to know something about me that I didn't. She was a very spiritual person, and her words were always very encouraging. While in the hospital, she showed a great deal of personal motivation which seemed to rub off on the others around her. This helped me get involved in many of the group activities, even though I was so deeply depressed.

One of my special talents is writing. At the time, I had already been published several times and had a great deal of recognition. I soon started sharing my work with many of the other patients, and they were very impressed. Even the staff members were impressed. It felt great to be recognized again, not only as a writer, but as a human being.

I was soon released from the hospital, but as I stated earlier, the adjustment period was just too much for me to handle. When I told this new found friend over the phone what a hard time I was having, she mentioned a support group which she had been attending called Emotions Anonymous. I asked her clarifying questions, such as: "What is this group all about?" "Will this group really help me?" She replied, "The only way to find out is to attend an EA meeting." Once again I knew this woman was steering me in the right direction, and somehow I knew I would be forever grateful.

I took her advice, and to this day I still remember that first meeting. I was very nervous, but I was also very optimistic, hoping that this would finally be the place where I would get the help I so desperately needed. I didn't quite understand what was going on in the proceedings because I was unfamiliar with the structure, but I was aware of the general sense of well-being among the participants. I was also surprised to see so much enthusiasm and, most of all, the driving desire of the group members to get well. These people had been exactly where I was right then, and they had no intention of going back.

As the group sharing continued I became more and more nervous. Finally it was my turn to speak. I just sort of trembled as if about to say something, but nothing came out. I passed, and in the process, I learned my first slogan, "This too shall pass." After that I sighed with relief and felt much more comfortable just listening to the others speak on the step or story we had discussed earlier in the meeting.

After the meeting the same woman I mentioned earlier must have noticed some uncertainty on my part about my willingness to return, so she said to me, "Give it at least six weeks, and if you're still not sure, we'll give you back your misery."

When I got home that night I started to think about my first depression and how miserable I had felt. The event occurred a few years after graduating from high school. Immediately upon graduation, I had been fine. I had a lot of friends, a job where I was able to make ends meet, and, other than the job, no major responsibilities. I didn't attend college, although I knew I had the ability if I wanted to apply myself. Instead of pursuing a vocation, I took a vacation from the real world and shunned the few responsibilities I did have. I needed to find myself, to find the real me. I wanted to escape from reality, but all I found myself doing was stalling for time. I did nothing but hang out at bars and lounges. It was great until all my friends started to drift away. I got used to simply hanging out, I really didn't have any direction or path to follow. I had no idea what I wanted, so I continued to hang out, still searching for the real me.

During this period of my life I had no idea who I was. I became very lonely and depressed. I started drinking more heavily until I reached the "pint" of no return. Everything started to fall apart. My whole life was deteriorating before my eyes, like an old structure about to topple.

Finally that structure did fall and things seemed to change for the better. I felt good again, perhaps too good; in fact, I had never felt better. This led to my first manic-episode; although, at the time, I had no idea what was taking place. The depression had lifted, and after so much suffering over the previous months, this feeling of euphoria really felt great. I was full of life and energy, moving nonstop. I didn't let anything or anyone get in my way. I became very flamboyant, going through my entire bank account. I had even joked with the teller, telling her that I had just suffered a severe depression, and that at the time, I was experiencing withdrawal symptoms. With my happy-go-lucky attitude, she found this information hard to believe.

Suddenly I became a rude, obnoxious, and very belligerent person, but I still had that wonderful feeling of euphoria. Once again I found myself in the psychiatric unit of a suburban hospital. Thereafter, I continued to experience states of depression and manic-episodes, all requiring hospitalization. I was hospitalized so many times the psychiatric unit where I was staying seemed to have a swinging door. On the outside of the door was the sign, "Manic-Depressives Only." Underneath that line it read, "Do Not Disturb . . . Any Further."

After going over these dreadful experiences in my mind, I knew for sure I should return to EA the following week. I also followed their advice and kept coming back. I still attend EA meetings regularly.

I started to feel good again, but didn't experience the euphoric feeling I had before. Instead I felt peace within myself and with the people and things around me. I learned to live with unresolved problems, enjoying each and every moment. My life was no longer an emotional roller coaster. I actually felt that sense of stability which I had been seeking for many years.

I developed self-awareness by doing a daily inventory. I did this by reflecting on my character defects at the end of each day, picking out the ones I needed to work on. In Step Four I did a complete inventory and discovered that one of my biggest character flaws is impatience. That defect alone can lead to fear, anger, and guilt—three of my biggest nemeses. Every night I pray to God, asking Him for patience. I say, "Lord, give me patience, and I want it now!"

Step Two is where I really learned about God. I now consider God to be my Higher Power, after years of disbelief. I used to pray to God only when I needed things. This reminds me of a story about an old man who desperately needed money: He started praying to God, saying, "Lord help me win the lottery." Still no money! Finally he said,

"Lord, are you listening to my prayers?" The man heard the voice from Jesus saying, "I am listening to you, and I heard all your prayers. I would love to help you out, but you have to buy a ticket!" Of course this story is only an analogy, but it's a good one. In Step Two I learned we are not handed anything, and we really have to believe in something before it comes true. Before EA, I had no faith at all and didn't believe in anything. I had no goals or direction; in fact, I had no guidance whatsoever and no path to follow. Now all that has changed because I have found something to believe in.

I now have goals and ambitions. One of my biggest goals is to keep on writing because this is a God-given talent, and it is a good way for me to express myself. Through EA I have received a lot of encouragement. Besides being published in the *EA Message* magazine, I have also written a lot of humorous and inspirational pieces which I shared with the group on numerous occasions. I have become a role model to others in the group. Since I have undergone a lot of pain and suffering, and these people have always been there for me, I feel it is my turn to pay them back by sharing my experiences. I now can be a positive effect on the other members, especially the newcomers.

My keen sense of humor has created an atmosphere of fun at EA meetings and in my social life. I became involved in many EA activities by using my creative talents. I wrote songs and sketches for the EA Christmas party and the 1993 convention, which was held right here in Chicago.

Most of all I learned a great deal about myself as an individual person. I learned how to forgive and forget by making amends. By making amends I got rid of a lot of guilt feelings that seemed to build up inside of me. How do I spell relief? A-M-E-N-D-S! I also learned that EA is a 24-hour program, which plays a very significant role in everyday living. I have been attending EA meetings for the past five years, and I will continue to do so in order to maintain the sense of stability which I now possess. Since joining EA I have not been hospitalized. I can honestly say this is the best I have felt in my entire life. I finally found the real me, and I like what I see. For that I am forever grateful.

I've Come Home

Dian

I came into Emotions Anonymous through the back door. I attended family week at a drug and alcohol treatment center to "help" a family member. Helper of others, people pleaser, a woman who borrowed her identity from others — I had been found out; my masks were revealed.

Counselors at the treatment center helped me see that I needed help. I began attending Al-Anon and later open meetings of Alcoholics Anonymous. Here I was given my first experiences in unconditional love and acceptance. I heard many people at these meetings sharing their problems and how they were using the Twelve Steps to better their lives. For the first time in my life, I felt like I wasn't alone for many of these people were telling my story. However, the part that puzzled me was they could genuinely laugh. I wanted what they had. They told me if I kept coming to meetings and worked the steps I could find the happiness I was so desperately seeking.

My first year of meetings was mostly topic meetings. I learned a lot about myself and saw a lot of recovery in the people who came to the meetings, but they kept talking about working the steps to get their recovery. This baffled me. A lady in our group guided me to a meeting that was strictly a step meeting. That is when my recovery truly began.

However, in these alcohol-related meetings, there was always something missing for me. I felt different because I was not an alcoholic, did not come from an alcoholic home, and was not married to an alcoholic. Weren't there people like me with problems like mine who didn't have an alcohol background?

I received many wellness catalogs in the mail. In one I saw a book entitled Emotions Anonymous. Could it be there are people like me? I ordered the book. When I received it, I read it from cover to cover and began sobbing. I felt like I had come home. There are people like me! I am not different; I am not alone. I called EA in St. Paul to ask where the closest meeting was held. It was 340 miles away! I was devastated! I also received information from St. Paul about the Loners EA program and I joined that immediately.

With the EA Loners program and a couple of years attending other twelve-step meetings, I felt led to quit my job and make amends to my children by being at home more with them. I was to find out that my job had become my identity. For six months I slid deeper and deeper into a depression. I developed severe pain in my left shoulder, did not sleep or eat much, and could not make even the simplest decisions. I obsessed for months about wanting to die but did not tell anyone. My depression deepened. It scared me so much that I went to my minister who recommended a counselor.

I began counseling and found I was in a clinical depression which is a physiological chemical imbalance of the brain. My counselor sent me to a psychiatrist to get anti-depressant medication. He explained that I needed to take care of the physical chemical imbalance so that I would have the energy to work with the psychological problems that led me to this depression. I was extremely fearful of taking medication as two of my siblings had been addicted, but I was so desperate that I went to the psychiatrist.

The psychiatrist helped me understand that an anti-depressant for me was like insulin to a diabetic. It was not an addictive substance. It was a chemical that lessened my depression because my body was not making enough of that chemical. As my depression lifted somewhat after about four weeks on the medication, I had more energy and clearer thinking to work with my counselor. Taking anti-depressants has been a continued part of my recovery. Working with a counselor, taking medication, and going to twelve-step meetings gave me the support I needed to face myself and work the steps.

I had been encouraged by my Loner Sponsor to begin an EA group. I had never led anything in my life, and I was so fearful. I remember thinking, "I'm at the bottom already; there's nowhere to go but up." I read in the EA book a failure is someone who never tries, not someone who tries and does not succeed. EA was born in Rapid City.

A couple of months later I attended the EA International Convention in Minnesota for support. I came home with new ideas and with a sense of unity that I was part of a big and beautiful family of people recovering from emotional problems who were learning to live with unsolved problems and find peace of mind.

In EA I found people who loved me just the way I was. They even loved me when I was hurting, depressed, lonely, angry, or sad. This was new for me. I was used to only being loved for what I did — a job well done, good grades, a clean house, or how I acted — kind, friendly, or caring. My typical reaction when people asked me how I was prior to being in EA was to paste a smile on my face and say "I'm fine." That was the "public me." At home I was overly controlling, nagging, and would find myself sometimes exploding at my young children over the smallest things. This produced guilt and remorse, but after a period of time, I would find myself blowing up again. I was powerless over my emotions.

In EA I learned feelings are neither good nor bad; they just are. I came to realize I was suppressing what I now call uncomfortable feelings (i.e., anger, fear, self-pity, resentment, etc.). I began talking about feelings at and after my meetings with program people and reading a meditation book that had writings on feelings to help myself identify what I was feeling. When I became angry with people, I would share this anger with a neutral person. This enabled me to calm down, practice expressing my anger in an honest but not a cutting manner and then follow through by talking to the person I was angry at. I also learned to ask myself, "How important is it?" This often diffused my anger.

In our EA meetings, we studied the steps. The fourth step was a giant stumbling block for me. I did my first fourth step after being in the program three years. I was very critical of myself because of this. After all, many others did their fourth step sooner, and I felt I should be able to. This is when I used the saying, "Don't compare." In looking back, I see I needed to work the first three steps and work the assets part of Step Four before I could write on my character defects without becoming depressed. I heard in the program if you are having problems working a step, go to the step before it.

Step Three asked me to turn my will and my life over to the care of God as I understand Him. The God of my childhood was a critical, judgmental God — always reminding me of how bad I was. How could I turn my will and my life over to that? I realized the group and the love I felt from the people in it were my Higher Power. Could God be like them and not like my childhood perception of God which I had learned from my family and church? Slowly by exploring feelings with my sponsor, my counselor, and my pastor (who preached love and grace, not sin), I came to believe in a loving God.

My next step was what I call building my identity. In a meeting I heard "God doesn't make junk." I laughed and said, "Yes, he does, he made me." Learning to accept I had good qualities was a long, hard road for me. I went to many meetings a week, retreats on learning to love myself, and enlisted the help of my program friends to begin to believe not just in my mind, but in my heart many things I liked about myself. It took years, but I was making progress.

I was now ready to write on my fourth-step inventory with some pain, but not severe depression, as I now had assets to balance out those character defects. I was not all bad; I had some good too. Because of my perfectionism and my fear of Step Five, I kept my first fourth step simple and followed up with a more thorough one the next year.

Setting up my fifth step was another major part of my recovery. I was fearful of rejection. I was filled with guilt. My old thinking told me if someone *really knew me* they would know what a *bad* person I really was. I set up my fifth step with my minister, a very non-judgmental person. My pain and my desire for recovery were stronger than my fear, and I now had the support of a loving God and my EA friends. I did my fifth step! What a relief! I learned that too much guilt had caused me to exaggerate my shortcomings. I learned that making mistakes is a part of life. I joined the human race. My fifth-step person gave me a hug when I left. I drove into the hills to spend some time alone and experienced a nearness to God and a sense of freedom that I had never felt before. A saying I had heard in many meetings, "The Twelve Steps work if you work them," was becoming a reality for me.

During my years in EA, I have learned to love and accept myself *just the way I am.* I am loved because I am me not because of what I do. Feelings are now expressed openly in our home — both comfortable and uncomfortable feelings. My marriage has become a close, loving relationship (much improved from the blaming love/hate relationship). I am close to my children. I have made many amends to myself and others thanks to Steps Eight, Nine, and Ten.

I still depend on my meetings. They are a time to remember where I have been, a safe environment to feel whatever feelings are going on in me, a weekly honesty check, a place to watch people grow which encourages me to grow, and a place to show my gratitude by being there for the newcomer because I know "To keep the program, we must give it away." I am reminded to thank my loving God for Emotions Anonymous and this new way of life. I not only found the genuine happiness and laughter I was seeking; I found myself, love, acceptance, choices, tears, a loving God, close relationships, and a whole lot more.

I Am a Survivor

Jackie

I grew up in a large midwest city. When I was five we moved to a house in the suburbs. We attended church every Sunday. From everyone else's viewpoint, we were the perfect American family. The problem was they never saw my family behind closed doors.

My two half-sisters were a lot older than I. My oldest sister left home when I was very young. My other sister was often in trouble and spent a lot of time in detention centers, so was seldom home. My father worked three jobs, so he was rarely home. My mother was sick with "nerve problems."

When I was an infant my mother wouldn't care for me because she never wanted me. (She told me every birthday how dumb I was for not dying when she tried to abort me.) I was fed and cared for at night when my father came home.

My mother had a lot of anger built up from her past, and I soon became the object of this anger. The verbal abuse was daily. I grew up hearing I was stupid and worthless, and that I would never be able to live without her.

The emotional abuse was hard on me. If anyone would hold me on their lap or give me the nurturing I needed, I would be beaten for it later. I would come home from school to find my room cleaned out with everything in the trash cans outside. I learned I couldn't be loved. I learned not to trust people.

I cannot say when the physical abuse started, but I know it ended the day I left home. It was done under the name of discipline. When I came home from school, my mother jumped out from behind a door and started hitting me. I never knew what I did wrong. My sister would come home late, and I would wake up with my mother beating on me. Her reason was so I wouldn't do the same things my sister did.

The sexual abuse started when I was young, and at first it was just my mother. Then her brother started. Next my mother started planning and supervising intimate parties for one other little girl and me. We would dance close to slow music and end with sex. Her reason for all of this was that I would never be more than a prostitute so she was getting me ready.

Throughout my life my father did nothing to stop the abuse. In grade school I had very poor grades so the school sent us to see a psychologist. My mother convinced him that I was stupid and she was A-okay. In junior high the school psychologist started seeing me. He believed what I told him but said, "You've made it this far. You can make it until you are eighteen." I did make it, but when I was eighteen I was so wounded and broken I couldn't leave because I believed all I had been told.

God had other ideas, however. I was removed from home by some friends who never believed my story until the night they saw my mother beat me. At last I was free! At least that's what I thought. The physical and sexual abuse stopped that night, but the rest just kept on going. Even when my parents disowned me, the messages (the old tapes) kept going on and on in my head. I had tried cutting my wrists before I was five years old. I tried drowning these messages with alcohol. I decided pills would work better. I tried many times and never could die. Here I was an adult who couldn't trust, couldn't love, didn't know a thing about my sexual identity, and couldn't get rid of the pain inside.

When my parents decided to start talking to me again, I got even more messed up. Again God found me a new family to show me some new ways to live. This family moved west and encouraged me to move too, so I packed my bags and moved one thousand miles from my parents. The move didn't cure me, but it freed me from the continued abuse by my parents.

I still tried to die a few more times which led me into therapy. One day the therapist said, "Why don't you try Emotions Anonymous?" The closest meeting was one hundred miles round trip. I drove to it three times, but was too afraid to go in. The meetings were held in the same building as the psychiatric ward. Walking into a room of strangers in the same building in which I had been locked up as a patient filled me with fear. Fear that I would walk in there and never get out. Fear that when I walked into this room of strangers the whole world would know I was crazy.

At last the courage came, and I went through the doors. What I heard I couldn't believe. Everyone said a little piece of my story. I thought I had found the way — that in twelve weeks I would be well! Twelve weeks came and went; in fact, now years have come and gone. I am still not well, but I am not as sick either. I still get depressed, but I no longer have to try to kill myself or stay in bed for days or weeks. I can just be feeling down and still go on with life.

I can accept the love people give me, and I can love others. Trust is built very slowly, and I am very careful to build friendships with only trustworthy people. At last I can build trust, and I have a few people I feel very close to.

I am currently a nurse who cares for others who hurt, not a prostitute like my mother said I would be. I can even take care of myself. Death is no longer the only way out. I now have other tools to use when the old tapes start playing. I have the steps to use to help me climb back up to life. Each time I climb back up it gives me more strength to keep walking with the knowledge that I am a survivor, not a victim. The steps tell me I don't have to go it alone. I have a Higher Power to give me strength and guidance. Step Nine gives me hope as I read the promises and see them coming true for me. The slogans give me something short to keep repeating in my head during those hard days. They also fill my head with positive thoughts instead of all my regular negative ones. One slogan is especially true for me, "I need people" because I have a tendency to isolate myself. The people of my group are the ones who support me through the hard times and rejoice with me through the great times.

My life is not problem-free, but it is free. I am free to be who I really am. I can laugh — not just because I should, but because I really feel like laughing. I feel the joy of life.

Many times after that first EA meeting, I would fall into the pit of despair and feel I could not get out. However, EA and my Higher Power (God) were always there to support and encourage me to take the risk and try life again. The group members would remind me of the slogans "This too shall pass" and "Let go and let God." Most important, the others in the group accepted me as I was and just kept sharing with me. As time has gone by, my downs are now only potholes in the road of recovery. The deep pits are in the past.

People often ask me, "If you could, would you go back and change your life?" My answer is no. My childhood was painful and the recovery from it has been hard, but all of this has made me who I am today. I am not a victim but a survivor; a survivor who enjoys life and is willing to meet all of life's challenges as a chance for new growth.

I no longer see or hear from my parents because I do not need to be abused anymore. I now belong to a very large, nurturing, caring, and loving family. They are my family of choice. EA is part of my family. To leave my family of birth was a hard choice because I was taught to "honor your father and mother." I decided it was a choice of them or me. The day I made the choice of me was the day I knew I truly loved myself.

This is in no way the end of my story, but if I had to write the end, I hope it would go like this: With my family of choice by my side, I meet each challenge with a zest for life.

I HAD TO ACCEPT BEFORE I COULD RECOVER

Vicky

I was born in 1952, the youngest child in a family of four, and raised in a small town in Iowa. My family has a history of alcoholism, depression, color blindness, and mental illness, so I was born with a genetic predisposition to manic-depressive illness. My brother became an alcoholic, and I developed manic-depressive illness.

My father abused alcohol and nicotine when I was a child. My mother was a caretaking co-dependent who enabled all of us. I was verbally, emotionally, and sexually abused as a child. I was overweight, had poor eyesight, and crooked teeth. At home the message was, "What's wrong with Vicky?" and, whether or not my feelings had been hurt, this caused me to be very sensitive. More emphasis was placed on how I looked than on what kind of person I was.

As a child I did a great deal of reading — sometimes as many as twelve books a week. I learned to escape through reading, writing, drawing, music, and eating. I ran to the refuge of the library, church, school, my aunt's family, my friends, and other people's houses. My aunt's family seemed more like my real family.

During high school I abused alcohol and concentrated on having as many dates as I could. This made me feel worthwhile. I began to excel in extracurricular activities and studies.

I went to a private college and became a hippie art major. I finished college in three years, worked part-time, graduated magna cum laude with a grade point average of 3.89. I earned a teaching certificate and began to travel.

I took a job teaching art in western Iowa. I married my college sweetheart, an intelligent man my own age who I thought was sure to succeed in life. We moved to Kansas and later to Georgia. He got a doctorate, and I got a master's degree. We abused alcohol and other drugs throughout our ten year marriage. I became angry because he seemed to be succeeding more than I was.

In 1980, I was twenty-eight years old, which is the typical age for the onset of manic-depressive illness. I was teaching full-time and being a foster parent for a young man with cerebral palsy whom my husband and I had taken out of an institution and into our home. I was beginning to work on a doctorate. All this produced a great deal of stress.

It was late summer in Georgia, and I had my first manic episode. I quit teaching and felt like a failure. I did not understand what had happened to me. Had all the stress caused a nervous breakdown?

I began playing in a band. I went to law school, but dropped out after two months because of anxiety and the beginning of another manic episode. I had my second affair, and my husband was so enraged that I feared for my safety and checked myself into a psychiatric ward.

I did not realize I was in the grip of a mental illness that would tear my life apart and make the next seven years a blur of manic episodes accompanied by terrifying delusions and hallucinations, followed by hospitalization, over medication, and depression. This caused feelings of failure and guilt about these manic episodes. I began rebuilding my life slowly. Believing I was cured, I discontinued the medication, becoming hypomanic and then acutely manic again. From 1980 to 1989 this disruptive cycle repeated itself over and over again five or six times. My life became the roller coaster that is typical of the cyclical nature of this illness.

After four years of my manic-depression, my husband wanted a divorce. I was devastated, but once again I began the long process of gradually rebuilding my life. I became manic again, was put on lithium, gained fifty-five pounds, and felt once again like a total failure. Not only did I have this mysterious emotional problem, but I was now divorced and fat.

I began life on my own, a journey that would lead to recovery. I taught public school and college in the Ozarks and began to concentrate on my spirituality. I attended twelve-step groups and studied yoga. I went to New Zealand to study and teach. Once again believing I was cured, I discontinued my medication, became manic, and flew back to the states. In Los Angeles I was handcuffed and taken to a psychiatric hospital. I was overmedicated, became depressed, and was flown back to Iowa with a social worker accompanying me.

But this time I did not feel like a total failure because I had followed my dream of going to New Zealand. I knew more about spirituality now, and I was beginning to get some insight into this mysterious illness. This time I did not have to rebuild all of my life.

I began to research manic-depression, chemical dependency, and mental illness. While reading a pamphlet on dual diagnosis (mental illness and chemical dependency), I encountered a reference to EA. I knew there were twelve-step groups for emotional problems. I was excited to learn about EA because I had bottomed out with emotional problems five or six times in nine years.

I wrote to EA asking about the Loners program and meetings for me to attend. Through the Loners program, I met my sponsor and began to really work the Twelve Steps for the first time in my life. We also worked through the slogans. We shared a lot about what was going on in our lives. I was dumbfounded that my sponsor was never shocked about the things that had happened to me — five hospitalizations, divorce, problems with the police, problems on the job, and failure experience after failure experience. She was never offended by the things I wrote. She never gave up on me.

I began to be more open with others about my past which was very healing for me. Instead of hiding my emotional problems, I began to try to solve them. Before EA, my hospitalizations had been cloaked in a secret pocket of shame which I carried around with me. Now I could open up to other people, and no one was shocked or offended or walked out on me because I had such a terrible past. This was great! I felt like other people understood where I had been. Above all, I felt like the people in EA accepted me — mental illness and all. This helped me learn to accept myself and forgive myself which was the real germ-seed of recovery. I became aware of all of these people across the country and the world who are in recovery for alcoholism, emotional problems, compulsive overeating, etc.

The last time I was hospitalized was in 1989. I continued to research this mysterious and destructive mental illness which I have. After joining EA I continued my therapy and seeing my psychiatrist. I read a great deal about manic-depression and learned that it is a lifelong illness from which I can recover, but for which there is no cure. From EA, other reading, and personal experience I have learned it is possible to recover by medication regulation and compliance, participation in twelve-step groups, therapy, seeing a psychiatrist, reducing stress, abstinence from alcohol and drugs, and the help of my Higher Power, who is God.

EA has helped me in so many ways. My sponsor and I worked through the *Step by Step* booklet. I was able to face all my character defects squarely for the first time in my life. When I made amends to people in my past, I felt as if a great burden had been lifted. It was as if I had been repressing a lot of pain and unfinished business for years. Repressing this garbage from the past was a terrific waste of energy. With each amend I made I felt lighter, freer, more energetic, and more in today rather than in yesterday. Through EA, I have developed a closer relationship with God, and I find myself turning things over to Him more readily all the time. What a relief to know I do not have to deal with problems on my own any more. I can share my successes and problems with the accepting folks in EA and with my Higher Power. I have learned to express my feelings appropriately rather than keeping them inside. Today I owe my emotional health to EA. I feel very grateful for all the help I have found through EA in coping with life's stresses.

First, however, I had to accept that I have a mental illness. Then

I developed a strategy which has worked successfully for four years now. When I become hypomanic I consult with the psychiatrist about increasing the medication slightly which short circuits an acute manic episode. This self-discipline and knowledge is not easy for a person with manic-depression. When I am feeling great and am productive and elated, the last thing in the world I want to do is take a tranquilizer. However, if the hypomania is not short circuited, it will develop into a full-blown manic episode and tear my life apart.

From 1980-1989, I bottomed out five or six times with my emotional problems. Each time I was released from the hospital, I felt like a complete failure. When I finally accepted that I have a lifelong illness, and I can recover but not be cured to the extent that I no longer need medication, I began to recover. For five years now I have been with my boyfriend, and we are very happy together. For four years now, I have not been in a hospital and have been able to short circuit the acute mania by regulating my medication with the help of my psychiatrist and by using self-discipline and knowledge about the course of manic-depressive illness. For three years now, I have worked successfully full-time at the same job helping troubled adolescents. Now I have stability and security instead of chaos and guilt.

Finding EA helped my recovery immensely. Step One pointed out my powerlessness over my emotions. I had to *accept* that I have a mental illness over which I am powerless in order to begin to recover. I continue to progress in being freed from the fear and anxiety that has caused so many problems in my interpersonal relationships. I now acknowledge and express my feelings rather than denying, stuffing, and distorting them. Through EA I have learned that there are many people who have emotional problems. I no longer feel weird, unlovable, and isolated. I thank God for EA and for one more day of sanity.

The Tapestry

Linda

I woke up in ICU on Tuesday around 10:30 a.m. Not until my husband and children walked in did I realize someone had found me. My first thoughts were anger. It was my only suicide attempt, so I made it good and covered my tracks well. The last time I was awake was 8:30 p.m. on Monday. After that, I remember nothing. Someone found me around midnight, and I was unconscious for over twelve hours. My family did not receive very much encouragement from the emergency room doctors. My worst fear had happened. Someone had found me. I was alive and would now have to face people and a great deal of them judgmental. Not only that, I now had to be committed to the psychiatric unit. What a horrible realization. I had seen a therapist before but never a psychiatrist.

It began with my battle of anxiety attacks. Even my family, especially my family of origin, could never realize how devastating the attacks were. The resulting depression with the downward spiral effect made me feel scared, inadequate, like I was going crazy. After ten years of these anxiety attacks, mainly kept in secret, I decided that *no* life would be better than living with the pain. My husband and children would be better off without me. But God had different plans for me, and now I had to go on.

After three weeks of hospitalization and intense therapy, I was discharged with the promise that I would join an Emotions Anonymous group. Discharge was on Tuesday last fall, and on Wednesday, I drove alone (an accomplishment) to my first EA meeting.

The contact person for the group was warm and welcoming. She explained that I should come to five or six meetings before I made a decision as to whether or not this was the group for me. Wise advice! The group kept talking about working the program; however, I did not understand what that meant. Finally, on my third visit, I purchased the EA book. I couldn't believe how encouraging it was to read the first few chapters. It was hopeful to discover that there were so many people with emotional problems and that it was possible to recover. The endorsements were heartening and promising. There were people out there who suffered like me. There were people who understood. No, I wasn't alcohol or drug dependent. I neither drank nor used drugs. No, my husband wasn't an alcoholic. Our three children had not presented us with any unusual problems. Also, I do hold a very responsible full-time position at a large place of employment. (I did take one month off work after my hospitalization.)

I was, however, co-dependent — nurturing others and taking care of everyone's needs but my own. For almost fifty years, I buried everything that I thought might displease others deep inside of me. Any unacceptable thought, feeling, or outward expression was intolerable. The price tag for this coping mechanism was high. For years I avoided dealing with feelings and unacceptable thoughts. I kept very busy and would not allow these feelings any space. It was like putting a bandage on an uncleansed wound. But the wounds festered, and I kept bandaging them because it was too frightening to clean them by working on them. I didn't want to be put under a microscope. However, the feelings no longer allowed themselves to be suppressed. The result? I begged God every night to take my life. Since I couldn't cope, the only answer was to remove myself.

Through hospitalization, therapy, and my EA group, I now have all the tools to get better. I would like to be able to say it has been an easy journey all the way. There have been a few setbacks, however, and that's okay with me now, for I have learned these are not only normal but necessary to healing. When I am in a setback, such as having fragmented thought patterns, justifying why I shouldn't be living, thoughts that I would never be a whole person again, and fear of going into a permanent relapse and becoming non-functional, it would be so easy to give up. However, my EA support group is there for me relating similar experiences and encouragement that I would not be stuck there. Comforting and hopeful are the words that describe the feelings the EA members communicated to me. I have also learned not to compare my progress with others. I can only compare where I am today with where I was a few months ago. Also, where I am is where I am supposed to be.

Is getting well hard work? Yes, harder than I thought. Nobody can do it for me. It means being committed to taking care of myself. It means taking the time to journal and identify feelings. It means working the Twelve Steps, such as sitting down with the EA book and reading the steps one at a time and seeing what I need to do to get well. Challenging! It also means, to be introspective to a helpful degree, but not to the point where I am stuck there refusing to look at available options. It means becoming aware of feelings and thoughts that surface and dealing with them on the level exposed to me. It is then my choice to ignore those feelings or acknowledge them even though this process may be very uncomfortable. Ignoring the feelings hinders my progress. They will not go away until they are dealt with. It means reading recovery material and attending EA meetings on a consistent basis. It means not letting my feelings dictate my behavior. It means accepting that I will always be in a state of recovery.

Is it worth it? Yes, healing is progressive. You see, I know what it is like to wake up in the morning and before I even get out of bed, feel my heart beating so loudly it resounds in my ears. I know what it is like to be afraid of my own thoughts—feeling fragmented. I know what it is like to feel I am going crazy. I know what it is like to want to be *whole* again. I know what it is like to lose touch with my feelings. I know what it is like to cry every night and beg God to take my life.

Has EA been responsible for my progress? Have I made any progress? To my amazement, much progress has been made. I have received promotions at work, and I feel fully functional. Entertaining others in my home is now becoming as easy as it was at one time in my life. As I drive to work I reflect on how I thought I would never be this functional again. When I think of all the things I am able to do now, I would like to encourage others not to give up. Yes, discouraging times come, but so do the encouraging ones. In the back of my journal I write down those accomplishments I never thought possible. It is helpful to read them and share this information with others in EA.

Emotions Anonymous has given me a new hope, a new inspiration, a new way of thinking, and a new way of life. I say "thank you" to those who have made EA possible, and "thank you" to God, who evidently isn't finished weaving the tapestry of my life.

EA – I Had to Check it out

Tillie

In 1974 I was reading a book which referred to Emotions Anonymous in St. Paul, Minnesota. The name of the organization triggered my interest in checking it out. Perhaps it was something from which I could benefit.

My emotions were not the greatest as I was solely dependent upon others for my happiness. The friends I had were those of my mother and my sister, really none of whom I could claim as my own. I feared for my future. I thought of a distant relative who lived and then died in a mental institution. The family never spoke of that person. Could my life end that way too?

I obtained a St. Paul telephone book, looked for the Emotions Anonymous number, dialed it, and had a surprise! A kind, compassionate lady answered my call. There actually was an Emotions Anonymous! I inquired about the organization and where a meeting might be. She gave me the location of a group nearby.

That very night I attended my first EA meeting. When their turn came everyone introduced themselves by saying, "I'm _____, and I am powerless over my emotions." My turn came, but because I thought I could control my emotions, I said I was having trouble with my emotions. No way would I say I was powerless – at least not until my fourth meeting. I decided, "Heck, I'll say it the way the others do!" I said my name and "I'm powerless over my emotions." A heavy weight seemed to be lifted from my back. For the first time my mouth was verbalizing the truth about myself – I cannot control my emotions! The only control I have is in how I react to my emotions.

Was this really a group of members who were anonymous? One

lady in the group referred to conflicts with her spouse. A gentleman there also made references to differences of opinion with his mate and how the EA program helped in solving the problems. It took a year for me to discover they were husband and wife. Yes, there was anonymity in this group!

My first eighteen years were spent growing up on a diversified farm. For that, I am grateful. There was always something which needed to be done. At thirteen I was given sole responsibility for one facet of farm life, but I was also learning many other things: gardening, canning fruits and vegetables, cooking, killing and dressing chickens, cleaning barns, milking cows, driving the horse during haying and later on, driving the tractor during harvest time. One year I was even paid by a neighbor for being in the strawstack to pack the straw while the threshing was in progress.

My social life in those years consisted of the 4-H Club and church related activities.

It was during those childhood years that my lack of self-esteem began. My low self-esteem partially resulted from being a year younger than my classmates in school. My peers were ahead of me. I finally asked my mother, "Why did you start me in first grade when you did?" She explained my constant begging to go to school induced her to comply to my wishes. I attended the one-room elementary school. I never did catch up to the others until I had been out of high school several years and went back to continue my education. Today learning is important to me, be it in a classroom or by other means. Learning is fun.

I do have one regret. I wish my parents had taught me the art of taking inventory of our family *positives* and how fortunate I really was. I would not have wasted my time being envious of my peers who seemed to achieve more, to have prettier clothes, more friends, a more carefree life, better grades, exciting experiences, more fun, et cetera. I could have been proud of my own achievements and would not have been jealous of my friend when she canned a quart of peaches all by herself, but would have remembered I had been canning peaches *all by myself* two years before but had not mentioned it to anyone. In those years I felt what I did, did not seem as important as what others did. I still find it hard to mention my achievements and to be assertive in what I believe. It is so easy to believe my ideas and successes are irrelevant and revert to my old ways. Now I have the tools of EA to not let that happen. No one can make me feel inferior nor can they make me feel happy. I do that to myself.

It was the idea in Concept Twelve of who you see at the EA meeting, what is said at the meeting, stays at the meeting and is not to be repeated to anyone that started my recovery from the guilt, shame, and feeling of inadequacy which resulted from incest. I did try once to tell an adult, but my childish faltering way of expressing myself was not heard because it took too long for me to say what I needed to say. I felt I was to blame. Did I encourage it? Did I enjoy it? Was it my fault?

When I finally said *No* and refused to cooperate, the incest stopped. However, the self-abasement, low self-esteem, feelings of inferiority, guilt, and shame, as well as the feeling of *I did not deserve* did not stop. They continued on until EA entered my life. It was after I quit hiding by acknowledging it to the group and in a one day EA meeting speech that I found I was not alone. Several ladies came to me after my talk to share that they too had suffered similarly. I have discovered the defects and secrets I had harbored for so long were not unique to me. Others have had them also.

After being in EA for six months, I took my first fifth step. I was afraid to tell the truth, but the person assured me there was nothing which would shock or surprise him. I found that hard to believe. Prior to EA, my experiences had been not to tell anyone — to keep things private — thus protecting myself from the gossip which would surely evolve.

Prior to joining EA, the idea of taking my own life had also entered my mind. Because it would be wrong and imagining the trauma it would cause whoever would discover my lifeless body, I reasoned against it. The feelings of worthlessness still do recur at times, but never with the same intensity as before. It is when I set unreasonable goals for myself that I set myself up for feeling worthless.

I give credit to EA for strengthening my faith in a Higher Power. I always believed I would be punished for all my wrongs. Now I know my Higher Power is a loving God who accepts me as I am. It is wonderful knowing my Higher Power is available to me at all times.

Another fringe benefit of EA is the number of friends and acquaintances I never would have had if I had not been an EA member attending EA events. The members come from all walks of life, but in EA everyone is equal in that we are all powerless over our emotions.

EA has become my lifeline. It provides all the necessary tools for handling my successes as well as problems. Few stories surprise me or shock me for I have heard them before. I intend to keep attending the weekly meetings as long as I possibly can because I am still *checking it out!*

Meetings Are for Me

Candy

My name is Candy, and I'm powerless over my emotions. I had known long before ever hearing about Emotions Anonymous that I was powerless over my emotions: the crying, emotional binges, excessive worrying, and panic attacks. The hard part was admitting I needed help and could not get better on my own. Having a panic attack in my living room, all alone, was when I hit my emotional bottom. What was next? Hiding in my bed under the covers? It was time to use my ace in the hole, a two-year-old newspaper clipping on a meeting for agoraphobia. I asked my husband to place the phone call. The meeting had been changed to an Emotions Anonymous meeting. Little did I know that this meeting was to change both of our lives.

I had two conditions which had to be agreed upon by my husband. He had to come and sit beside me, and I could leave if I started to feel uncomfortable. He agreed.

At the first meeting, we sat in the back row nearest the door. It was a speaker meeting. The woman standing up front amazed me. As she told her story, I hung on her every word. How could she be so open with this large roomful of people. I was overwhelmed and grateful. We stayed for the entire meeting. Standing and holding hands, they closed with the Serenity Prayer. I was a little afraid of the closeness, of holding someone's hand. I didn't know anyone, except my husband. Joining the big circle, I remember the power of the group.

During successive meetings, I heard, "Take what you like and leave the rest" and "God of my understanding." I especially like the slogan, "I have a choice." Realizing my vulnerability, these were assurances I needed that the program truly was a spiritual program and not a religious cult.

Many times I would look forward to the meetings all week and then two hours before the meeting, panic would set in, and I would not want to go. I probably used every excuse from the weather to needing my rest. My husband was undaunted and would literally drag me out of the house.

Once I refused to go to the meeting so he said, "That's okay, but I'm still going." This was a bombshell. The meetings were supposed to be for me, not him! My husband was my support person. When he got back that night, I wanted to know who was at the meeting and what was said. I was told if I wanted to know, I would have to go to the meeting myself. He was following Concept Twelve: ". . . at meetings we can say anything and know it stays there. Anything we hear at a meeting is not to be repeated to anyone." I definitely did not like that answer. I began to worry that maybe my husband would pick up the tools of the program faster than I would, that he may get better and I would be left behind. I knew I was missing out. I needed to go to the meetings if I wanted to learn the program and find peace of mind. I would not be able to do it through my husband.

In the beginning, I could not say my name or participate in the reading, let alone share my experiences. I was afraid of making a fool of myself and crying. I was able to talk briefly with members at the break or after the meeting. My sponsor told me not to worry, that in time I would open up.

Feeling the need of another outlet for the pain I was going through, I went to a psychologist specializing in short-term treatment of stress and anxiety. The sessions with him were very helpful. He encouraged me to keep going to EA meetings. There would be no instant cure or short-cuts. Meetings were my answer.

On looking back, not being able to talk at the meetings was the best thing that could have happened to me. For the first time I began to really listen. Many times, I could hardly sit still during the boring readings at the beginning of the meeting. Then, hearing them read over and over, Concept Four started sinking in, especially "We do not judge; we do not criticize; we do not argue." I began to trust and to share. Now, I know why the readings are included in the format.

Part of my social phobia was being easily hurt by what others said. This sometimes included comments made at a meeting. Crying in the car on the way home one night and saying, "I'm not going back." This was taken in stride by my husband. He said, "So you got shot down, no big deal." He reminded me we are all in EA because we need help. I needed to remember *principles before personalities*. The program asks for honesty. Sometimes, I had to face myself and admit the other person was right and then take action. Other times the comment was off the mark, and it was best to let it go. To begin accepting others and myself as we are made me less sensitive. I learned I don't go to meetings for another person, and I don't stay away because of another person. These spiritual awakenings were disguised as rude awakenings.

Now that my husband was going to EA for himself, I began to compare my progress with his. I tried to be more like him and keep up with him, even though we were complete personality opposites. I was doomed to fail. I became more depressed. Then came Steps Four and Five.

The fourth-step inventory was a real eye-opener. It was easier taking my husband's inventory than looking at myself. As much as I wanted to be like him, I began to see how critical I could be of him. In *my book* Concept Six read, ". . . and not try to improve or regulate anybody except *my husband.*" The Serenity Prayer reminded me that I could not change another person, including my husband.

The time had come to take an inventory of myself. My first inventory consisted mostly of negatives. I was still comparing myself to others. The fifth-step person I saw helped me become aware of my good qualities. Adding them to my inventory list, I found a realistic balance.

With my husband and I attending the same meetings, I began to learn a lot about him. This was good. At home I did most of the talking.

His answer to "How was your day?" was always "Okay." Then, I would talk for an hour about how my day had been. At meetings we all have an equal chance to share. Now I try to practice this principle at home.

Several years passed. With more meetings in the area, getting to them was still my biggest hurdle. I always felt better once I got there and started seeing the others arriving. After the meetings, I unquestionably felt better. I kept reminding myself of this as it came closer to the time to leave my home. I would not want to miss out on the tool of the program that was meant for me from that meeting.

My husband and I moved from Massachusetts to New Hampshire. I really missed my old friends and meetings. How would I survive without them? I had attended the Derry, New Hampshire, meeting on frequent visits to see my parents. Now it was my only meeting. I asked my Higher Power for another, closer meeting. After my husband spoke with the VA Medical Center, they let us use a room. We placed a notice in the self-help section of the Sunday newspaper. I now had a meeting that was within walking distance of my home. Two months before, someone else had formed the Concord meeting. With three meetings a week my Higher Power had answered my prayers.

A short while ago, my husband asked me to take the key for the Concord meeting. He would be unable to attend three weeks in a row. On the drive up to that first meeting the old panic set in. It is a long drive, not many would be there, and I still had my other meetings. These were all good excuses for not making the next two Concord meetings. First, I would ask my Higher Power to get me to this meeting. Then at the meeting, I would give the key to one of the other members. I had a choice, didn't I? Good, the pressure was off. Just as I felt the old anxiety slip away I thought, "I'm going to really miss the next two meetings if I don't go." I had another choice. I no longer needed excuses. I would make plans to go to all three meetings and encourage the newcomers to keep coming back. This happened two weeks before my tenth year in EA.

What a difference! My old attitude had been "poor me, why do I have to be the one going to meetings? What did I do to deserve this punishment?" Today meetings are a gift. I could not have made this change using my own willpower. It came as a result of attending many meetings.

What about being too tired to go? It may be that I have not paced myself during the day. Putting the meeting on my to do list and prioritizing are helpful. I also tell myself "easy does it" throughout the day. When this fails to work, I remind myself of my emotional bottom, of how it was before EA. I can take it easy and have energy to attend the meeting or I can tire myself out and still attend the meeting. Either way, meetings are for me.

In time (my sponsor was right), I have come from not being able to say my name at meetings to sharing during the meeting and to chairing meetings. I have also been able to attend international conventions. Some of the twelfth-step service I have done has included setting up chairs (even someone who doesn't talk at meetings can set up chairs), ordering literature for the group, being the group treasurer, representing the local chapter at intergroup, and taking on various secretarial duties. I am currently serving one year as president of the intergroup. By becoming a trusted servant, I am giving back some of what I have gained. By pitching in I am helping the meetings to continue. With meetings I will keep growing. Someday, I hope to tell my story standing in front of a roomful of people.

I am grateful to my husband for taking me to meetings, for knowing when to let me make the decision to go, and for giving me that key. Without him and the first meeting in Quincy my story would be very different.

Has my husband picked up more of the EA tools than I have? EA has finally taught me not to compare. We are different people on the same journey. I am working my program, and he is working his. That is what counts.

There's Nothing I Can Do

Verna

There's nothing I can do. That was my theme song prior to joining the EA program. Since others were causing my problems, nothing would help unless they shaped up. Self-pity and hopelessness were my constant companions. Although I was physically abused as a child, my parents were good people. The problems of life were so overwhelming for them, and they could not handle having me around as a child.

The physical abuse wasn't as bad as the hours-a-day of verbal abuse — the shaming and the belittling. I needed to be assertive, but I learned that it wasn't safe. My parents hardly ever let me go elsewhere to play or have friends over to *drive them crazy!* So I never learned to be assertive with my peers either.

I thought maybe I should try to please my parents more, but that only made me into a doormat. Years later the *Today* book would give me the words to describe this problem. The May 1 meditation talks about "protecting my sense of well-being." That is what I could not do, and I didn't have a clue of how to go about it.

I found safety in isolating myself from everyone. Every encounter with others that went bad was further proof there was safety and comfort in isolation for me.

I had many physical symptoms which doctors couldn't treat — stomach trouble, nasal congestion, being cold, and always being tired. It was like a big hand had me by the back of the collar and was holding me back. I had one hope — that any day I would find the magic that would change all the *others.*

I acted out my bad feelings by not doing the things that would make my life orderly; such as, not being ready on time, not doing my school work, not having my clothes in order, and, as an adult, not doing housework. In this way I hoped others would see how bad they were making me feel. My life remained chaotic, but there was *nothing I could do* except review my miseries and blame others.

I didn't trust anyone. I thought people should be so nice that they wouldn't hurt me, and I didn't think this was an unrealistic expectation. When they were not as I expected, I decided they wanted me to feel bad. At that point I would go into self-pity, be safe and not try to be assertive.

I saw a number of therapists over the years. I learned about books, tapes, speakers, classes, and workshops. I tried most of them, but they weren't enough. They did not give the things the EA program does.

I came into EA in 1981. The first gift I received was warm, caring, and accepting people who treated me with respect. They did not minimize my problems or tell me how I *should feel.* They spoke of a God they felt good about, not the God of fear and punishment that I knew. I was impressed with these people and began to feel hopeful. I couldn't believe I could be so lucky as to find this wonderful group – and I could go there every week!

At EA meetings I learned I couldn't change other people, but I thought that was what had to happen. When I heard "pain is inevitable, suffering is optional," I didn't believe it. Members said, "Change your way of thinking." I thought that meant to pretend the bad stuff doesn't matter. I had tried that before, but to no benefit. They suggested I be more assertive, but that made things worse, for I only wanted to avoid conflict.

It took me a long time to find enough of the EA tools to get started with my recovery. Meetings, retreats, program friends, the *EA* book, the *Today* book – all helped me feel validated. I used the *Today* book like a textbook, looking in the index for the subject that was troubling me. If I didn't find it in the index, I added it in the margin and filled in the pages as I found them. The readings often inspired thoughts which I wrote in the margins or took paper and journaled about them.

I found I was not wrong to want my life to be better. The bleak world I was seeing was not all there was. I learned about a healthy life and thought it might be possible for me.

Gradually I started to make decisions in my life. I stopped trying to have peace at any price. If that caused an altercation, I was ready. I was learning how to be more assertive without anger. Sometimes it didn't seem to make a difference right away, but a few weeks later I would find that things were going better. I was also learning patience.

I stopped letting others decide what I *should* want and who I *should* like. How freeing that was! What a relief it was for my resentments! More and more often I found I was feeling so much better and concluded this must be serenity.

Recently I have come to realize what was hindering my self- esteem. I thought the increase of self-esteem would take away my pain. When it didn't I discarded the whole idea. I came to realize there may not be anything that will take away my pain, just allow it to be more bearable. Now, when I start down my self-pity path, I focus on what is okay about me. I know there is no way focusing on the negative will make me feel better. I now work at meeting my own needs and no longer blame others when they do not meet my needs.

My Higher Power now goes with me on my journey; I am no longer alone. He helps me see what I am contributing to my problems and helps me be aware of what I can change. Everyday I pray to know what God's will for me is except in the "dry times" when it is difficult for me to pray. I ask for the strength, courage, willingness, self-discipline, awareness, and humility to carry out His will. I ask for special help with self-discipline and awareness.

Accepting His will is no longer a problem since I read in the *Today* book, August 26, that God's plan may be better than mine. Many of my plans haven't been so good. God helps me steer more carefully and not fall back into the old ruts as often.

I often pray for God to help me think clearly, not to panic if I start feeling discounted or not listened to. I picture God standing beside me with his hand on my shoulder — being with me. He helps me avoid being immobilized with self-pity. He helps me see the program with a new awareness, seeing things in the steps I could never see before.

An amazing thing has happened. I now have the energy and willingness to do my housework! I have a long way to go in dealing with some of the chaos in my life, but each job I get done is something I can feel good about.

Sometimes when I am needy, taking action seems too difficult, and I think I will never get to where I want to be. Then I remember where I started from and how much I do not want to go back there. Then I get back to working my program.

The second Just For Today is one I focus on, "... my happiness does not depend on what others do or say or what happens around me." It helps me let go of external events and work at getting my needs met. It is when I am needy that I depend on others to do and to say what I want.

"Look for the good" helps me overcome years of magnifying the bad. I can look at the whole picture instead of a few unpleasant parts. Reviewing my miseries cannot make me feel better.

The people at meetings help me remember I am not alone and help me get things in perspective. Sometimes it is tempting to skip a meeting, but I need what I get at meetings — the warmth and caring, the chance to listen and be listened to. I need those things.

I ask for God's help with many things, even those I used to think were too trivial. Often within five minutes, I find a good course of action to deal with the problem. Sometimes I have to take smaller steps than I would like to, but I keep on. I will keep going as far as I can get.

Whatever the outcome of following the program may be, it will be far better than what was going on prior to joining EA.

No Questions Asked

Ron

My story is not a pleasant one. It is very difficult for me to tell, but it may help you on your journey to serenity. At times I have been ashamed of myself. I feel bad about parts of the past and wish certain things never happened. However, I cannot undo the past. I can only live with today and go forward. I want very much to do that.

At eighteen I attended a local university, majoring in education. I was a perfectionist and worked very hard to maintain near perfect grades. In my first year of college I met my wife-to-be, and we were married in the spring of 1975. I did my student teaching in the fall of that same year.

I taught school for three years. The first teaching experience was finishing the school year in a fifth grade class in our city's school system. It was a bad experience. I was the third teacher in the classroom that year. There were plenty of wild students.

I changed to another school system in the hopes it would be better. It was better. In fact, by the second year in this rural school I actually spent much of the weekend looking forward to Monday.

The old, rural school was set for demolition, so I transferred to another school within the system. I was to teach fourth grade and coach the middle school football team. I was very nervous because I didn't know what to expect. The school reminded me in many ways of my first teaching experience.

At this time my wife became pregnant with our first child. I tried to carry my burdens. I prayed to God. I wanted to be the *perfect* teacher, husband, coach, and father-to-be, but the load was too heavy. I began to lose sleep. In fact, nights would go by, and I wouldn't sleep. My lack of sleep led to some delusional thinking and hallucinations. I tried to get help and counseling.

A low point in my life came when my wife and I drove across town to admit me into a hospital. I did not want to live. I honestly think that without my wife's belief in me, I would probably not be alive to tell this story.

In the hospital, days turned into weeks, weeks into months, and my wife continued to visit me and carry our baby. My condition did not improve even with all sorts of drug therapy. In my state of mind I viewed myself as a hopeless case. Finally my doctor released me from the hospital, as the baby was due at any time. I was not much better mentally, and I suffered depression for many more months to come. Four months later I was hospitalized once again.

My new doctor removed all my medication, and I struggled to return to a somewhat normal life. I took a job in a machine shop and also worked a second job. I started to improve by working on my own at *blanking out* the past experiences. However, I continued to feel alone. How I wish I had known of EA back then.

Now it had been eight years without medication, and eight years of slow progress. We decided to have a second child. I handled my wife's pregnancy very well, and I was beginning to feel normal, like everyone else.

The added expense of two children made it necessary for me to find a better paying job. I obtained a job in a tool and die shop. The pace was faster, hours were much longer, and expectations were higher. I was in a groove of fifty-five hour weeks that became a trap. I felt I could not shorten my work week in my position, and after two and a half years in this pressure cooker, I snapped.

At that point I ended up in the hospital in isolation. This was the absolute lowest of the lows in my life. It was worse than the first hospitalization because I felt that those ten years of hard work to get better were lost. I was diagnosed as unipolar depressive and eventually medicated with lithium and navane. I wanted my life to be better but had absolutely no idea of how to achieve it. Eventually my privileges at the hospital were increased, and I noticed a flyer advertising Emotions Anonymous. The meeting was on Wednesday night in another area of the hospital.

With my background, you can imagine my hesitancy to attend, let alone talk. What I found with EA has quite literally helped me not only to survive but to improve emotionally over these past five and a half years. Not one single question was asked about my background. Everyone seemed so friendly. I decided to attend the next week and the next. Eventually I became a regular, and I began to turn my problems over to my Higher Power. I started to find a little peace of mind, however small. I loved this group and consider them to be my roots in EA.

I returned to the pressure cooker job I had before my hospitalization and the discovery of EA. Through the help of the EA program I have made changes in my work attitude which has brought me some serenity. I keep a copy of the *Just for Todays* in my tool box for needed inspiration from time to time. I am especially fond of "Just for today I will try to live through this day only, not tackling all of my problems at once." It reminds me to handle the problems at hand first.

I have found it helpful not to compare my work performance with others in my department. I try to give an honest day's work, but I don't compare it with others. These ideas which I found in the EA program are my survival skills proven on the job.

Working the steps has been important to my emotional progress. In my ill state of emotional health I hurt many people. I made amends to them all. Some people I wrote to and expressed my sorrow in having hurt them. This proved to be an important step in healing our relationships. I feel better communicating with these people now.

When my work hours changed to second shift, I initiated a new daytime EA group. Recently I have returned to the Wednesday night group where I discovered EA. The EA members there have given me courage to continue to work on my emotional health. I plan to continue to attend the weekly meetings.

I feel like an automobile on the highway of life. Occasionally I must come in for gas, oil, or a tune-up. I have tried to make EA a service station for my emotional health. At EA meetings I obtain encouragement and my emotional road map that I need for this trip called life. When I had my breakdown, EA provided the proper mechanics and parts to put me back on the road to recovery.

When was your last tune-up? Is your gas gauge nearing empty? Are your emotional tires wearing thin? Time to check your belts, hoses, or oil level? Don't try to do it yourself. Full service is always available at your local EA meeting. Come on in! Life's journey and your road to recovery will be simpler with regular maintenance.

I cannot predict the future. I do, however, feel positive about my progress since finding EA. Emotions Anonymous has provided a program that encouraged me to live one day at a time, turning the things I cannot handle over to my Higher Power. My hope is that this story will lead you to attend EA meetings, work the steps, and turn it over to your Higher Power. This is my experience; this is what has worked for me.

Thank you EA and the members of that first Wednesday night group. You were so accepting and friendly. I dedicate my story to my Wednesday night group. Through the EA program you have made my progress possible — one day at a time.

I Was Afraid of My Fear

Jerry

My name is Jerry, and I am a neurotic. I was born during the depression of the thirties. My family was dirt poor. Even though we always had food to eat, sometimes it was bacon grease sandwiches or cornmeal mush for supper. We had no idea what luxuries were. My parents did the best they could to bring us up in what they considered to be a hostile environment. I can remember my father was very judgmental and my mother was always afraid something might happen to us. I learned these lessons well, and I too became a very frightened and judgmental person. I always felt everyone else was better than me.

To counteract my poor self-esteem, I developed pride in my ability to take charge of any situation and get things done. I always felt I knew better than anyone else how to do it, and it was anything I set my mind to. I was able to show my teachers shortcuts in problem solving, especially in math. I was very anxious for the approval of others. Once, as part of a group of travelers we were caught in a blizzard while driving over the southern Rocky Mountains. To prove myself as the one with courage and superior ability to take charge, I drive the car to safety.

By the time I was twenty-three years old, I began to experience moments of strange feelings. I experiences fear of ordinary things even though I knew intellectually there was nothing to fear. My chest pains and palpitations felt like I was going to die. That's when the anxiety attacks began.

I went to the doctor about my symptoms. After a complete examination, I was told "I can't find anything physically wrong with you." They always emphasized that word *physically*. I got to know many doctors personally after that, for I felt I had to find the cause of this malady which was robbing me of enjoying my life. I can remember one time I had the doctor test me for abnormal blood sugar. I was actually hoping I was physically sick so I wouldn't have to admit that I was emotionally sick.

I was very fearful of many things, but most of all I became afraid of my fear. I felt completely alone and thought I was the only one in the world who felt this way. I went to a psychologist who told me he had never heard of anyone being afraid to drive on a freeway. I knew it! I was the only one!

My fears kept closing me in, and I built myself a psychological jail about two miles square. I felt if I had to cross one of my limits I would die. I became afraid to go to church or to a restaurant. I couldn't go to the dairy case of the supermarket because it was at the back of the store. It was too far from the parking lot. My fears are too numerous to list here. I was simply afraid of life on life's terms.

I tried to escape the pain of my fear and panic by running away from what I thought was the cause. I was afraid of the freeway, so I avoided the freeway. Any trip of more than a few miles was too far from home, so I avoided that. I had anxiety attacks when I went to church, so I tried to sit at the end of the last pew next to the door. Even that was too much anxiety, so I had to stop attending. I became an expert at blaming everyone in sight for my problems.

For a couple of years, I used alcohol as my medicine. I thought it helped, but one day I took a drink so I could get to work and it caused me to have a panic attack. This happened three or four times, and I had to give up the alcohol. I was still suffering the torture of anxiety and panic, but I no longer had the alcohol to get me through them. This was about five years before I entered the twelve-step program.

For about seven years, I used and abused prescription tranquilizers, taking up to seven a day, sometimes even trying to wash them down with beer. I was desperate to stop the pain.

I believed in God, but I was sure God was keeping a record of my wrongs and would somehow make me pay for all my sins. God was just one more thing I was afraid of.

I was in such pain that I thought suicide was my answer. I thought I would be in hell if I killed myself, but felt it couldn't be any worse than the hell I was living here and now.

It was at this time that one of the men in my office asked me if I had heard of people using the Alcoholics Anonymous program for help with emotional problems. I was so desperate for help. I had tried medicine, alcohol, exercise, vitamins, religion, and hypnotism up to that time. I must have also read four or five psychology books. It was like I had been in a dark room with no hope and now a light was turned on. I reached out for it like a drowning man reaches for a floating log.

That day I began my journey to emotional sobriety and spiritual wholeness. It was, however, a little rough getting off the ground. With the help of a member of Alcoholics Anonymous, I started a group even though I was as sick as any other newcomer. The only other group member was, Theresa, a lady who forced us to stay on the steps. If any childish or humorous activity would arise in a meeting, she would quickly and loudly tell us we were there to prevent suicide and breakdowns and ask us, "What step are you working on right now?" Because of her question, I went through the first five steps in five months.

Those months were really hard to get through. I think if it wasn't for the *Just for Todays* and the slogans, which I call the one-liners, I don't think I could have made it. Many times I had to tell myself "this too shall pass" or "let go and let God" to make the difference whether to face the day or run from it. It was then that I told my A.A. friend that the program was not working for me. It was working for others with depression, but not for me. He reminded me that people were telling me I was looking better and asked me to hang in there.

Within a month I was driving down the street and had a thought about driving into Los Angeles. Earlier that thought would have given me an anxiety attack, but it not only didn't, it actually felt comfortable.

At that moment I knew something had changed in me and in my thinking.

During the next month, I worked through Step Nine. I began to forget to take my pills. I had been taking six pills a day. I told my doctor, and, with his counsel, I was off the pills in two weeks. I have not needed a pill or any other mind-changing substance for over twenty years, one day at a time. The Serenity Prayer had become and still is my only tranquilizer.

I now look upon my experience of mental and emotional illness not as a liability, but as an asset. Because I was too weak to face life on life's terms, I had to stop relying on my own strength and seek the strength of a Higher Power. If it took my illness to bring me to that point, then I am glad I am a neurotic.

At my first meeting, I was the only newcomer and there was only one other in attendance — my friend from A.A. who was helping me to start the group. As he told me his story and the feelings he had gone through I was amazed to hear, for the first time, that I was not the only person who had these strange feelings. This has given me an awareness of how newcomers feel at their first meeting. It is so important to know we are not unique in our illness.

Before this program, everything I tried, failed. My business ventures were so short-lived that they never got off the ground. When a modicum of success came to me, I did a job of self-sabotage so I wouldn't make it. I always blamed my failures on other people. After I became a twelve-step member, I had an amazing turnabout and my business became more successful than I had ever dreamed. I quit smoking, one smoke at a time. I became involved in the ministry of my church. I began to release my old and new resentments, and as I did I began to believe that I too was forgiven. I found that I could trust God as much with my shortcomings as with my virtues.

In my experience with the Twelve Steps, I found a new way of life where, unlike the old way, it was not up to me to manage my life better and the lives of others in my environment. I now know that as I uncover a defect in my character or some other manifestation of my selfishness, I can see its bad effect on me (Steps Four and Ten), admit to it in my life (Step Five), be ready to be rid of it (Step Six), and ask God to remove it (Step Seven). Steps Six and Seven relieve me of the bondage of self. I no longer need to work on the defect, but, instead, hold God before me as I see the positive change in my life (Step Eleven).

Today I experience a feeling I never expected in this life. I like myself. I have really learned that it is okay to like myself. In learning this I have also learned to let others like me. I have many friends. Before the program I only knew people, but there were almost none who I could truly call friends. Loving myself and loving others has not only been the biggest benefit of this program, I now believe *it is the program.*

I am a blessed child of God given the most beautiful opportunity any man can be given. I have unlearned all the fears, judgments, prejudices, and criticisms that separated and isolated me from my brothers and sisters. I have replaced them with love and compassion which unites us, and I came to the place where I can truly say . . ."*Our Father.*" I am very grateful.

Bipolar Disorder: A Modern Story

Peanut

I cannot remember a time in my life when I was completely free of mental pain. In fact, my earliest recollection of this pain goes back to age four. I remember laying awake at night so scared that I would instinctively nuzzle my face into my older sister's sleeping body. I thought this would prevent my thoughts from racing. What happened to start this reaction in my mind is not important. How I have chosen to deal with the intense emotions that accompany bipolar illness has been crucial to my maintaining a normal way of life.

High school was the worst time of my life. I was in a severe depression at the age of fourteen. On most school nights I would be up until 3:00 a.m., frightened, anxious, enraged, even hysterical. In the mornings I would have a heaviness from head to toe and would just make it to school on time, never fixing my hair or using makeup (that would have been impossible). Talking in front of my peers would reduce me to tears, so I would ignore the teacher if called on. The kids laughed at me when I did this. They thought I was funny — actually, it was a mask I desperately put on to save myself. Through all of this I could still manage good grades, maintain an active social life, and work at appearing normal.

Frequently my parents would have me in the emergency room because of anxiety and psychosomatic symptoms. The doctors all agreed my problems were psychological. I would cry to my mom and tell her I really felt the symptoms. She would always be compassionate. We then came to the conclusion that the doctors were wrong, and I did not need any counseling.

My symptoms kept recurring throughout high school and college, and then again this pattern came to haunt me in my thirties. By then I was experiencing weakness and pain in my joints as well as neurological problems. Because I would not admit I had an emotional problem and deal with it properly, my repressed emotions were transformed into physical ailments.

After more than twenty-five years of suffering, I finally admitted I needed to look inside myself for some answers. Blaming other people and circumstances in my life was not working.

A very sweet lady with whom I had been hospitalized invited me to go with her to an EA meeting. At that point in time I was hardly capable of communicating with others and had a hard time sitting anywhere for any length of time. The continuing support from my companion made it easier for me to keep coming back to meetings despite these problems.

The people at the EA meetings were at various stages of recovery. I saw people who looked as scared as I was, but there were also stronger people who had been in the program for five or more years. They all gave me the hope I needed to keep going.

I believe my manic and depressive responses are coping mechanisms I developed when I was very young. When confronted with a situation or feelings that were hard for me to tolerate, I would spiral upward or downward to a degree that is not experienced by most other people. Today, medication controls my defective physiological response — the chemicals that shift my mood quickly. EA has helped me get in touch with the feelings and situations I find difficult, so the extreme chemical response does not occur.

One concept I have learned from this program is not to force everyone to adjust to my own desires. Most people are not the way I want them to be. Before EA I was very judgmental of other people's opinions, actions, and shortcomings. That got my internal chemistry going! When I catch myself judging people today, I try to let them be who they are, even though I might prefer them another way. Sometimes this involves distancing myself from these people until I can finally come to grips with the situation. Having close friendships within EA has taught me a lot about accepting myself and my shortcomings. As soon as I admitted that I wasn't perfect, everyone else seemed a whole lot more loveable. It is then a lot easier for me to be accepting of other people.

Easy does it. I think I approach problems and tasks today with one-fourth the velocity than I used to. I had a very hard time starting projects. In fact, my usual response to an assignment was to pace the floor or to do everything else besides the task at hand. Today I will always take a moment to pray to my Higher Power so He can help me do *first things first.* That overwhelming feeling will go away if I just remember I have a program to structure me. Sometimes the sheer thought of my sitting still at an EA meeting will give me the confidence to complete a task that is making me go too fast.

One of the nicest book marks I have received says, "Easy does it. Only when we discard our need to be on top and accept our vulnerability do we begin to grow." This saying has helped me tremendously. It seems to be the solution to most of my problems. As I sit in EA meetings I sometimes stare at this bookmark while I am trying to deal with a problem. Just the suggestion that I need not be on top slows me down and puts me in a better frame of mind.

Much of my continued success at handling my illness is due to being an active member in EA. When I first joined, an EA member asked me to take over the literature position in our group. Being very withdrawn, I knew I had to do something for myself. At first, I was quite shy, but slowly I became more confident. I started getting *out of myself.* One thing led to another, and, before long, I was helping with EA picnics and Christmas parties. EA offered me a golden opportunity to practice my social skills so I would not feel so awkward in my relationships with family and co-workers after my hospitalization with my illness.

There are still times when I think I can handle it all on my own. My independence and stubbornness can push me in the wrong direction. I watch for these feelings because they are warning signs. I am on the wrong track when I don't read any EA materials or when I don't call anyone when I need someone to talk to. I have to remind myself that God is my Higher Power, especially when I experience a mood that gets more and more expansive. EA has been excellent in *shrinking* my mind and helping me to turn a lot over to God.

I am very grateful for EA and all its members. It literally saved my life. Now I know I am not NUTS (Not Using the Tools and Steps). With EA, and the help of my Higher Power, I hope to lead a full and productive life.

No More White Knuckles

Carol

I had to move cross-country to find the healing power of the EA program. The family move was made because of a job opportunity for my husband in Phoenix and to avoid those midwestern winters.

I had begun having panic attacks in my mid-twenties and even had done the unthinkable in a small town — sought help from a psychiatrist. The doctor dispensed pills and was very expensive, which only added to my feelings of being weak and being a burden.

I was terrified to leave home alone for fear I would meet someone I knew, and they would see through my smiling facade and see the fear inside. At times I wouldn't answer the door or the phone because I was afraid a shaking voice or trembling hands would give me away.

After the move to Phoenix, I consulted a psychologist and took tests, participated in psychodrama and group therapy, but to no avail. I felt completely inadequate as a mother because I could not attend school conferences or be a room mother because of my fears. An appointment with a doctor, dentist, or even a hairdresser filled me with dread. The supermarket, a line at the bank, any situation where I felt I couldn't leave if panic hit, was an ordeal. I worried constantly and was a hypochondriac. I felt as if I was *white knuckling* my way through life.

Then my Higher Power went to work. One night on a TV talk show, a guest was discussing a twelve-step program for people with emotional problems. Within a week, an item appeared in the Phoenix newspaper saying a meeting of this group was beginning within two miles of my home!

Oh, that first meeting! I was scared, but I stayed. Even after months of meetings, I sometimes would sit in my car in the parking lot and then feel so scared I would return home. But I must have felt some spark of hope, because I kept going back. I am sure a large part of why I kept going back was the fact that I felt no judgment of my emotional problems, and also because EA had a specific plan for getting better. That plan seemed overwhelming, but I thought maybe I could do some of it — maybe start with some of the *Just for Todays*.

We were neophytes and didn't quite know how a meeting should be run. This was before the publication of the EA big book, so we really had only the yellow pamphlet for guidance. We talked about our fears, anger, and depression, but never the steps. Since ours was a small meeting, it didn't take long to realize that all we were discussing each week was an update of our current troubles. We were going nowhere, and, besides, it was boring!

Because of a local newspaper story, suddenly we were deluged with new members. It was then we began to realize that a meeting where members discussed their complaints and various therapies was not working, and we began having step meetings. A friend had loaned us an A.A. tape, and the speaker mentioned that unless they worked the steps, their members were merely alcoholics who weren't drinking because their thinking hadn't changed. Since we weren't dealing with a substance, we were lucky enough to go straight to our thinking!

I was troubled by all the references to God. I guess I felt if somehow I was a good enough person, I wouldn't have been cursed with my emotional problems. Over the years, my relationship with my Higher Power has evolved. In the past, I had felt unacceptable to God, but the understanding and love I received from other members and from my sponsor who knew my deepest, darkest secrets helped me to realize the love of my Higher Power must be unconditional as well.

Through the steps, I had to face some hard truths about myself. I could own up to fear and depression, for I thought they were my defects of character. However, I painfully learned that control, perfectionism, anger, and resentment had major roles in my thinking. It was necessary to take an honest look at myself. The honesty of others helped to open the door for my self-honesty.

Step One had always seemed simple to me. Obviously, I was powerless over my emotions or I wouldn't be attending EA. It took a long time to realize that I came to EA to learn how to be power-full over my emotions. For me, the most important word in Step One is acceptance. I felt I would only be acceptable when my problems were under control. I didn't understand it was necessary to accept myself as I was. To me, that felt too much like defeat. Deep down I felt I was holding myself together, and if I accepted my fears I would disintegrate. How could I accept this person who was terrified of the world, who dreaded the future, who was hopeless?

Then I got a lesson in acceptance. Following brain surgery for an aneurysm, I developed a seizure disorder. I was told I would always have to take medicine to control it. Even using my strongest willpower and determination, here was something over which I was truly powerless. I sank into a deep depression. But thanks to what I was learning in EA, especially the idea that my Higher Power was in charge and I could trust that Higher Power, I emerged from that depression with a deeper understanding of acceptance. I don't feel my Higher Power punished me with an affliction; I feel I was presented with an opportunity for growth. This brought home to me the meaning of the Serenity Prayer, especially the part about granting the serenity to accept the things I cannot change.

Another important part in my ongoing recovery is service. I live closer than anyone to our meeting, but for a long time I would never take responsibility for opening the room, setting up, leading the meeting, etc., because that meant making a commitment. However, I began in small ways. I took the key and opened the classroom. I made coffee, put out literature, and talked to newcomers. Then I was taking EA phone calls, became intergroup treasurer, and served as an EA regional trustee. One year at the EA convention, I even volunteered to chair a Board of Trustees committee. A far cry from being unwilling to lead a meeting or open up the meeting room.

Service to EA has been an invaluable part of my emotional growth. Most of all it got me out of my self-centeredness. In the past when I was out in public, I would look at the people around me and think, "Everyone's happy but me." When I began to really know other people in EA and learned to be more honest with myself, I realized I truly wasn't alone — not in a *misery loves company* way of thinking, more a *we're all in this together*. I have never been involved with people who were so honest about their feelings which has been invaluable to my own self-honesty.

I now am much more comfortable with myself and others. I can do those things which seemed impossible for many years. I began by taking my Higher Power along when I was driving — just one traffic light to the next, and giving myself permission to turn tail and run if I wanted. Since the pressure was off, I did it — I got were I was going! I was even scared to talk at meetings. I would spend all my time there wondering if they would know I was scared. At an EA meeting! So I gave myself permission to pass when it came my turn to speak, so I could listen to what others had to say and be comfortable when it was my turn.

Then, solo trips to the grocery store, post office, and library — it was amazing! Rather than popping a tranquilizer before facing anything, I found after fifteen years I was forgetting to take them. I did carry them in my purse for a while as a security blanket. The person who was afraid of being in the backyard alone could now drive to the airport and fly to Chicago, along with my Higher Power. I never want to forget how it was because each day is still a miracle.

I wish I could adequately express my gratitude to EA and my Higher Power for restoring me to a functioning human being, for the love and patience of my family, for my sponsor who has seen me through thick and thin, and for the precious people I have met in EA who are such an important source of joy, love, and strength in my life.

TOO MUCH EXCESS BAGGAGE

Jack

My name is Jack, and I am powerless over my emotions. I came into Emotions Anonymous twelve years ago. Although my search is still incomplete, the twelve-step program has brought me an inner peace I would not have thought possible. I would like to share with you part of my life which encompasses my search for serenity.

My preteen years were relatively untroubled, but as a teenager I got into a lot of trouble. I was involved in break-ins and stealing from stores. We destroyed tires on about a dozen cars, destroyed a fence, cut down street signs and did many more things. I remember headlines in the local paper, "Vandals Strike Again!"— and that was us. There were many parties with drinking, and I was not yet sixteen. During this time and in spite of it all, my parents stood behind me, although there was a fair amount of discipline when I got caught. I only realized in later years how lucky I was to get caught for most of my misdeeds.

At sixteen I was sent to a large city to go to school. My dad told me, in all seriousness I am sure, "I'm sending you out of town before my best friend has to send you to jail." His friend was the town magistrate. Those three years spent at school were filled with a lot of drinking and partying. This behavior carried on into my working life.

My parents were separated that first year I was away, and they later divorced. I thought I handled the situation very naturally at the time, but I carried this trauma with me for many years. I considered myself very mature for my age.

I was married at twenty-seven and for the next five years carried on much as I had before being married. We had a son, and unbeknownst to me, my wife started having a very difficult time. But not me! I said,

"This shouldn't interfere with our way of life." For me it didn't.

My wife and I worked hard and saved our money in a very disciplined manner. We were able to accumulate all the basic material things — house, car, etc. Then we started to accumulate other material things that were not so basic. We had a cottage by this time and spent all our free time there. We bought one boat and then another bigger one and so on. I thought soon we would accumulate enough and we could start enjoying life. When we finally tried to take the time to enjoy our life, much to my surprise, I found I could not. I guess the enjoyment was in the acquiring or in the anticipation of enjoyment.

All of a sudden everything seemed to be wrong, or maybe I just became aware of an accumulation of wrongs. I had tried in the past to fill some nebulous void in my life. This emptiness followed me everywhere — at home, at work, with our son, and at the cottage. I tried many different things to fill this void — drinking, religion, fishing trips, gambling — but it only made me frustrated and angry.

In order to understand this strange void I had finally taken notice of, I started a journal. I would write some of the feelings and emotions I was experiencing and in this way try to express them.

I came to my first EA meeting with the idea that I had nothing to lose. I was quite angry with some of the members at this meeting, for they did not seem to belong. They appeared quite happy, and I could not fathom why these happy people were present at such a serious meeting. I took my depression very seriously, and I did not need these happy, seemingly frivolous people at this most serious meeting. I am grateful now to be one of those happy people.

For many months after I started going to meetings, I sat and only listened. For the first six months or so the only sharing I did was to say "pass." As much as I wanted to take part, I was unable to do so. Eventually, I learned that I could formulate my thoughts before the meeting, write them down, and then read them at the meeting. This helped me pay total attention to what others were saying instead of trying to think about what I was going to say.

I was angry at members who tried to help me — and at those who didn't. I expected someone to tell me what I had to do to feel better. But, since I didn't ask, very few volunteered any information. Fortunately, I was left to do my own thing. I had to find my own way to work the program because we are all different.

I think the one part of the closing statement which I heard at every meeting kept me coming back: "Through sharing and working the program to the best of your ability, you will find help. You can learn to live with unsolved problems and find peace of mind." I did so want to share and be absolved of all the things I despaired about. I also kept coming back because members were telling how they *had felt* and how they *felt now.* Those were the happy people I was antagonistic towards. They told stories that made my depression and the reasons for it incidental. I thought my problems were unique. If these people could live with their problems, then surely I, with only my small problems, could get help from this program. It felt like forever, but within a year, I, too, was able to experience a modicum of happiness.

Step One, admitting I am powerless over my emotions, is always important to me. This step continues to remind me I am powerless and it helps me to underline in my mind that I still need the program and must continue to work this program to the best of my ability.

Finally admitting to myself that I am powerless over my emotions was a traumatic moment in my life. I was sitting in the kitchen reading Step One. I had read this before, but hadn't really admitted this to myself. All my growing-up years I had been taught to be in control of my emotions and not let emotions control me. I continued to think that if I admitted to being powerless, I was admitting to being a failure as an adult and as a man. I always thought I could control the results if only I tried hard enough. I blamed myself for not trying harder. In wanting to work the program I felt I had to take a really hard look at myself as far as Step One was concerned. In looking at the way I reacted to events in my life, I finally realized my life, in an emotional sense, was indeed unmanageable. With this realization I understood I was powerless over my emotions. I remember the tears streaming down my face and going into the bedroom so my family could not witness my humiliation. However, after ten or fifteen minutes I felt a great sense of serenity and as if a great weight had been lifted from my shoulders. This was a real spiritual awakening — as I later learned to call these experiences. I now felt I had admitted to being powerless, and I could really begin to do something about feeling so miserable and perhaps begin to work the program. The road to my recovery began right here with this step. This became the beginning of hope for me that I, too, could benefit from this program.

Anger was the biggest character defect I was aware of, and I chose to work on this initially. This awareness came after about a year in the program. Anger was always a part of my life. In retrospect, I see that anger brought me pain and a sense of guilt. I believe anger had controlled a great deal of my life in the past. When I became enraged and lost control, I unwittingly handed over control to another person or thing. I also used anger to control other people, and it did work. I would lose my temper if I thought my shortcomings were too noticeable, and people would back off.

Having become aware of this through the program, I tried very hard to curb my temper. This certainly was not an easy task since it was a reaction that had become natural to me. I came to learn that anger, as an emotion, was okay and natural. However, I had to work on anger's control over me. I now try to control my reaction to my emotion of anger instead of letting my emotions control me.

When I got angry, I always wanted to get even. I have become aware that by doing this I hurt myself much more than the other person. While I am upset and losing sleep with thoughts of resentment and getting even, the other person is sleeping soundly, completely unaware of my turmoil. For me, patience and letting go overcomes anger and irritability.

My anger came disguised as many other things: intolerance, resentment, impatience, selfishness, over-sensitivity, vanity, sarcasm, distrust, anxiety, envy, indifference, silence, discontent, cynicism, self-pity, and jealousy. Some symptoms I came to recognize were: stomach pains, headaches, hypertension, digestive and intestinal disorders, and back and joint complaints. When I chose to work on anger as my primary defect of character, I had no idea all these other defects would come into play. Although I have slips with this list of defects from time to time, the success I came to have with anger brought me a long way on my journey in working the program.

There have been days during my recovery when just about everything seemed bleak and even hopeless. I allowed myself to become depressed and angry. I see now that it doesn't matter what I think, and it doesn't matter what I feel. It is what I do that counts. Now when I become anxious or upset, I try to get into action by going to meetings, participating, and working with others in the program.

I had allowed myself to move quite far from anything spiritual. I felt I should do it all myself. By coming to my first meeting I had admitted I needed help, but I realized later that I had not *let go* entirely. Relying on my own will, I did not have to trust anyone. I came to understand even later that I felt unworthy of a Higher Power's attention, but worse yet, what if I accepted a Higher Power and I was not accepted.

Before coming to the program I really had no concept of spirituality. I, of course, had heard of the Holy Spirit as it related to religion, but certainly not in reference to myself. I went to Sunday School as a child, but in one way or another, conned my way out of going. As a young man I searched for a belief to put my faith in. I went to different churches and read about religions, but was generally put off by most of them. I quit looking, losing faith in mankind as a whole, and if anyone asked, I declared I was an agnostic. The more history I read on how men had used the church for their own gains the more I became a confirmed atheist and would argue vehemently with anyone who cared to argue.

The program does not require me to accept a traditional religious concept of God. I am asked only to recognize a spiritual truth, that there *is* a source of power greater than myself. I can label it in order to talk about it. It is not necessary for me to be able to understand or define that power. The steps require me only to accept that the power is there and that it is available to me.

Since coming into the program, I have experienced real growth. My self-worth was truly low, and I was extremely lethargic. Being involved with EA has given me a new energy to enjoy life — no matter what my problems. Procrastination has almost ceased in my life, where before it almost consumed me.

All the good intentions in the world are just so much smoke if there are no actions behind them. EA is an action program. The steps keep me growing. I have come to realize for me to keep out of depression, I have to keep the program constantly in mind, and I cannot stubbornly work at the program trying to force an acceptance of serenity. I work some facet of my program every day, whether it be using a program tool on my own, going to a meeting, or carrying the message in EA service. In this way, I have found a continuing peace of mind.

Journey Toward an Effective Life

Kitty

I am a grateful member of Emotions Anonymous since August 23, 1984. I come to EA meetings to learn to live at peace with myself and to achieve serenity despite unsolved problems. I have learned I am powerless over my emotions. That is to say, they will affect me in some way no matter how deeply I repress them, how hard I try not to express them, or how fervently I ignore them. I have also learned that I do not have to react blindly to my emotions anymore. I have a choice, and I can choose a rational response to strong feelings. I have learned not to fear my emotions, but to appreciate them as guiding messages from my Higher Power which tell me when I need to change course in order to take care of myself.

I was a member of Al-Anon many years ago, and the Twelve Steps were invaluable in leading me to a sense of sanity in an insane situation. Before finding the program, I had made five suicide attempts, the last two being very serious. Working the steps helped me for the first time in my life to feel a wonderful sense of healthy self-esteem. I learned I could experience joy and real love, no matter what my external circumstances were. My marriage ended, so I no longer had to deal with the problem of alcoholism, but I continued to use the Twelve Steps in my daily life. They just made sense as a decent way of living. I attended Al-Anon until after I married again, this time to a non-alcoholic.

For several years, things went very well. I used the principles I had learned as a basis for daily life. My new husband and I moved from our tiny town to a large city in another state. We bought a house. I began attending college at the age of twenty-eight. Before the program, I was too insecure to attempt higher education. Now I felt able to risk trying new things and was confident of my abilities. I did extremely well, eventually graduating with honors. I started my career as a physical therapist assistant in home health care. Things were great! I had everything I had ever dreamed of — a wonderful husband, a nice house, financial security, an interesting career, and a good solid sense of myself. I was tremendously grateful for the twelve-step way of life.

But after a few years, I began to experience periods of depression. I was confused. I had everything, yet I was feeling awful. I suffered burnout at my job. I deluded myself into thinking if I went back to school for more training in my field, I would be able to do even more, and then I would feel better about myself. The fact that I was already an excellent worker and got much praise for the job I did just didn't penetrate my growing depression.

At that time, I also was serving on the board of the local branch of our professional association, but I felt like such a phony. I went to the monthly dinner meetings at very nice restaurants around town, but I really had no idea how to fulfill my duties nor the confidence to even ask.

I felt worse and worse about myself. I couldn't seem to use the twelve-step principles anymore. I knew I needed the support of people who were working the twelve-step program, but I no longer felt I qualified for Al-Anon. I felt very alone. In desperation to feel better, I quit my job, went back to school, and hid from life.

I hid out in school for a couple of years. I wondered if I needed therapy (I probably did), but I was too proud, too ashamed, and too angry at myself to go. I isolated myself more and more from friends and relatives. Our social activities almost ceased to exist. Most days I was so distracted by my misery that I couldn't remember to take meat out of the freezer for that night's meal. I dropped out of school. Most days I slept until noon or one o'clock. Then I would be up most of the night sitting on our screened-in back porch staring at the black night with thoughts whirling over and over in my head: "What is wrong with me? I have everything I want, why am I not happy? I used to know how to live life and now things are out of control. What if I get suicidal again? What the hell is wrong with me that I can't make the steps work for me anymore? I don't want to live like this. If only M— would shape up I'd feel better. If only my fantasies would come true and save me from this pit." I was very frightened, angry, and lost in fantasizing about wonderful changes rather than actually changing. I had lost all sense of my Higher Power's care.

During these futile nights on my porch, I yearned to return to the twelve-step program where I had learned to love myself and feel the care of my Higher Power permeating my days. But as I said, I felt I no longer qualified for membership.

One night I remembered having read a book years ago by a psychologist who had joined a twelve-step program for persons suffering emotional illness. It had been a very interesting book. I recalled at the time saying in my smugness to program friends, "Isn't that nice! They have a twelve-step program where the crazy people can go!" *Now I was one of the crazy people.*

I was seized with an obsessive hope that I could find that book in our local bookstore. I did find it, plus all the others he had written subsequently. I bought them all, took them home, and read for days until there were no more to read. I went back and began reading again, crying much of the time because I recognized myself on almost every page. I also cried because I feared the hope I was beginning to feel. I was afraid this Emotions Anonymous he wrote about would not be here in my city, and I wouldn't be able to *go home.* That's how I thought of it, as going home to the program, to a fellowship where I was welcome no matter what. The only thing I had to do to qualify was be a hurting human being who wanted to work the steps in company with others who were on the same path.

One afternoon I worked up courage to make some phone calls to see if there was an EA group around. I sat with the yellow pages and called every social service agency that might know about EA. No one had any information. I called hospitals and mental health clinics. They wanted to schedule an appointment with a psychiatrist for me, but no, they knew nothing about EA. I called the Alcoholics Anonymous central information number. They had heard something a couple of years ago about EA but didn't know where it was, if it was still around. Finally, one unlikely city agency had heard of EA and had a couple of contact numbers I could call. I was elated.

I diligently sat down each day for the next three days beginning at nine o'clock and dialed the phone over and over until four o'clock in the afternoon. Then I would quit, rationalizing that I didn't want to intrude on anyone's evening family time. Of course, I was really struggling with this idea of joining the group for *crazy people*. I was making sure to call when chances were everyone was at work. I never left a message on an answering machine because I didn't know how to do that, and I felt ashamed of that.

But the third day, a woman answered a little before four o'clock. I explained a bit about my twelve-step background and my current difficulty. She told me there were three meetings around town. She also invited me to the groups' summer picnic to be held in a couple of days. I didn't go to the picnic, but I did begin the next Thursday to attend EA meetings. I went to a meeting every Monday, Thursday, and Saturday for a year, then started a group on Fridays near my home. I went to all four meetings for quite a while.

At first, although I desperately wanted to go, I was afraid to come to meetings alone. My husband accompanied me, holding my hand to get me through the door. To tell the truth, I hoped he would find something at the meetings for him too, because I knew the power of the twelve-step program and how it had changed me before. I feared if he didn't at least understand what the program was about, I might lose him someday. My previous experience of working the steps was that my first marriage did not survive the changes. However, I had learned no matter what happened, with the program I would be okay. Thank goodness he did, indeed, find something for himself at meetings, and he, too, continues to attend EA today.

As I attended meetings, it didn't take long for me to begin to feel better about myself. It was such a relief to hear others share their experiences. I realized I was not alone in my wild feelings; I was not a freak or a shame to humanity as I felt. Within a couple of months, I began to be more open to social engagements. We went on a canoe float with a group of friends, and I was so pleased that I wasn't afraid of the people or of the canoe (I don't swim). I could hardly wait to share this story with my EA groups. Over time, I began to feel more peace of mind and more willingness to risk taking part in life again.

I became interested in what I could contribute to our EA community here in our city. I had always been uneasy talking on the phone, but I agreed to be a telephone contact person for EA, so I could help someone as I had been helped. I started the group on Friday afternoons which was evidence of my progress to accept responsibility and make commitments again. I felt involved in life.

By 1986, we had five groups in the city, and I suggested we start an intergroup. Enough people became interested that we had a meeting to determine how to organize it and what our purpose would be. I felt involved and valuable to the process, a far cry from my experience on my old professional association board. It has been a source of pleasure over the years to realize that I had a hand in starting something good that brought many people together in service and growth toward emotional recovery.

As I grew in my program, I finally made amends to my parents for many hurtful things I had done in the past. In Al-Anon I had not been able to do that formally. However, in EA I came to understand that I make amends for myself, so I can let go of the past and live effectively today.

My EA journey has not always been smooth. At times there has been great pain. However, the pain always led me to a deeper understanding of myself and an ability to let go of others so they can live their lives as they choose. There was a two week period a few years ago when I suffered panic attacks that lasted every day for hours until

I was exhausted. It was also a time of having my barriers stripped away so I had to depend on EA and my Higher Power to get me through. I found I was willing to suffer, if need be, for the sake of growth. It produced a deeper honesty as I wrote in my journal and exposed to myself my bedrock emotions of fear and unwarranted deep personal shame. The panic attacks, my unreserved reaching out to my Higher Power, and getting a sponsor who knew what I was going through were the start of my intense experience of inner growth. Eventually, I developed a sense of peace and love toward myself and an ability to let go of all that shame. Today I know I am a beautiful, beloved person, even when I can't consciously think so. I am very grateful for those panic attacks, as painful and frightening as they were.

Things are so different now. I am very involved in life, particularly in service activities for EA. I have worked for our intergroup helping produce special EA events so others might gain deeper understanding of themselves and their program. I have started new groups, have been a sponsor, have spoken at EA conventions, and have served on the Board of Trustees of Emotions Anonymous International. I am no longer that frightened, zero self-esteem, depressed, angry woman I was. Today I know there is help for me anytime I sincerely want it. There are warm and loving meetings I can attend, people willing to support me, and stimulating EA events where I can immerse myself in the joy of the program.

I am still powerless over my emotions and occasionally suffer a low mood, but my worst days today are vastly better than my best days used to be. I have a new life. The Twelve Promises are coming true for me. I am very, very grateful. I invite you to try EA for yourself. If you are even a little willing to work the steps, you will be amazed and gratified by the progress you can make.

My Implosion

Vivienne

My depression began when I was seventeen years old. It resulted in bad grades my junior year in high school, then it calmed down. My thought disorder began when I was twenty-two. It was sporadic for about four years, then a voice started talking to me about my conduct.

At age twenty-two I got married to a man who was mentally disturbed. He had abnormal attitudes about women and was very verbally aggressive towards me. Our marriage lasted three years before we divorced. We had one child.

After the divorce, I was having a relationship when a hallucinatory voice started to haunt me about my sexual conduct. This voice was to consume every unstructured minute of my day. I continued in the relationship for three years in spite of the voice. Then I broke off the relationship because I could not stand any more paranoid voices. I thought everything would get better. The voice just got worse until in 1977 I started to hallucinate and hear choruses of voices talking to me. I also thought that demons were trying to posses me. I became so strange that my parents, whom I had been living with, took me to a psychiatrist.

My psychiatrist put me on medication, diagnosed me as paranoid schizophrenic, and told me I had to take medicine and come to therapy for two years. I felt like someone had put me in prison. I was not a willing patient. It took six months of starting and stopping my medication before I realized I needed help. I stayed in therapy for two years and then was taken off the medication. My condition got worse. My doctor put me back on the medicine and also prescribed an anti-depressant, since I was sleeping a lot and had symptoms of depression.

I worked really hard in therapy for eleven years.

Finally I found Emotions Anonymous in 1988. I had tried another support program for the mentally ill and found it to be very abrasive. A friend of mine who was also mentally ill told me about EA. She wanted to go, but not alone. I told her I would go with her.

The EA meeting was very impressive. People told their stories of how they had changed. When it came my turn to speak, I told those people what was wrong with me and, if anyone knew how to cope with paranoia, would they please talk to me after the meeting. The only method I had for coping with paranoia was to sleep it off.

I had been attending Narcotics Anonymous since March of 1987 because I am a drug addict due to mental illness. The two drugs I abused were alcohol and marijuana. The alcohol made me more depressed and the marijuana made me more paranoid. I stopped using drugs and alcohol in October of 1987 and have been clean for almost six years.

I used drugs to get in touch with positive feelings. When I was not high, the only feelings I was in touch with were feelings like rage, hate, and anger. When I was high I could experience love, joy, happiness, and humor. When I got clean I had a very beautiful spiritual experience which left me with a sense of presence, peace, and serenity which has sustained me for the last five years. I feel I am not alone.

My EA sponsor taught me how to create a space in my mind and the environment so I can focus when I am paranoid. I find reading the EA book or another book which interests me can relax my mind so the paranoia goes away. That helps me to create a space in my mind. To create a space in the environment, I focus very intensely on one other person and enter into conversation with them. I talk about a subject that I am knowledgeable about and listen to what the other person is saying. All of the surrounding stimulation recedes into the background. Hopefully, the conversation turns into an interesting evening and enables my mind to relax through distraction.

My paranoia is precipitated by stress. When I am ill, I feel abandoned, a loss of identity, and a groping in the environment for someone to tell me what to do. On occasion I have found saying the first three steps to be helpful. I concentrate on accepting the meaning of each step. Truly, when I am psychotic, I know that I am powerless and that mentally and physically I am unmanageable (Step One). I have come to believe I can be restored to sanity (Step Two). Then I turn my will over (Step Three). My symptoms do not always go away, but I feel much more relaxed and protected. After saying these first three steps, I feel as if my Higher Power is watching out for me and whatever happens to me is His will. Since stress triggers my illness, relaxing in a prayerful state restores me to the sanity promised in Step Two.

In 1991 my depression went away due to the influence of my sponsor and my medication. We were talking on the phone one day when I was in pain feeling a lot of guilt. My sponsor said, "People who are mentally ill experience their pain a lot longer than the normal person does." At that moment, I had an overwhelming insight and was released from my burden. I realized I did not have to feel that way any longer. I had suffered for eighteen years, and that was enough.

EA has helped me tremendously. Now, I am experiencing one psychotic episode for about an hour a month. I am a housewife and a student so my life has some busyness to it, but also some times of quiet throughout the day. I have been married for fifteen years, and my husband has seen definite improvement in my mental health. I am much more alert, I no longer talk to myself in inappropriate ways, and, most of the time, I verbally respond to people when they talk to me.

The biggest relief is the release from the pain of my past. Now I am happy. I will always be indebted to my sponsor for her methods of coping with mental illness, her insights, and her wonderful guidance. We are very close friends now. She knows everything there is to know about me, and she accepts me. That has really helped my self-esteem. The support I have received from the friends I have made in this program, along with the friends I have made in Narcotics Anonymous, has totally changed my life. I will always be indebted to Emotions Anonymous for the quality of my mental health.

THANK YOU HIGHER POWER!

Bob

I was born and raised on a beautiful farm on the edge of the sandhills in central Nebraska. My family worked and played hard. My mom and dad were good providers. I enjoyed everything about nature, but very little of the farm work. I did very well at academics, enjoyed sports, and was moderately successful as an athlete.

My childhood was emotionally painful. I was insecure and shy. I cried easily. When other kids called me names, I would feel very hurt and embarrassed. When my father would scold me, I would feel very hurt and ashamed. When I did not win at sports or get the best grade at school, I felt I was less of a person than the other kids.

I believe now my childhood insecurity was pretty typical of most children. Having my own son, whom I can see has the same insecurities, has helped me realize my personality was inherited. My son has inherited much of my personality and is sensitive too. Time will tell if my own experiences and parental guidance will help him handle negativity better than I did.

My family only expressed feelings of unhappiness. Happy feelings were experienced but not discussed. We had to be on guard of appearing conceited. I communicated my pain through tears and then suffered in silence. I drew the conclusion there was something wrong with me. I tried to do the right things and gain the approval of others to still my feelings of inadequacy.

My grades in school were very good. School was easy for me. However, it always seemed as if there was one person smarter than me. This would cause me anguish as I struggled with feeling inferior to that person. It was the same with baseball and the other sports I played.

Someone was always bigger, faster, or a better player of the game. To me this meant I just was not good enough. As you can see, I was building a pretty healthy inferiority complex!

I was dealing with the same life situations and feelings most everyone has to deal with. Each of us is perfectly human; therefore, we are imperfect. Each of us has someone in our lives who is better than we are at just about everything. Again, my experience with my own son has been very educational. As much as I have tried to protect him, he too encounters these same situations. It helps me to realize life is bigger than I am, and I do not control it. It helps me understand I do not need to feel I am an inferior person.

My high school years pretty much paralleled my grade school years. I was shy and insecure around girls. I would feel embarrassed before I even talked to them and then would not even ask for a dance or a date. I remember my first kiss. Talk about a fearful situation! It took unbelievable courage to cautiously get the okay signals to embrace and kiss. It only lasted a second, and I am not sure it would even classify as a kiss. What a thrill for someone so shy though!

There was one new and important development in high school. I discovered the world of alcohol and how it could boost my ego, giving me the feeling I was somebody. I would have a few beers and feel cool. I was more accepted by the cool crowd. Girls were less scary to approach. We were having great fun partying, being reckless and rebellious, and bragging about last night's exploits. Then we would do it again as soon as we could.

I graduated from high school president of the senior class, salutatorian, and winner of the award for excellence in academics and athletics. Unfortunately, I still felt inadequate and inferior. I partied on.

I went to college, and what did I learn? I learned all about drugs and how to party with them. Drugs were another mood altering crutch. Now I had two crutches, alcohol and drugs, and I could really move in the fast lane. College did not last long, as I dropped out to party and work, in that order.

About this time the Vietnam War was beginning to wind down. I was informed I was about to be drafted, so I enlisted in the U.S. Army. I met some great people and saw Germany and some of Europe. However, my alcohol and drug abuse worsened, and I was really wasting my life away.

During my second year in the army, my dad had a heart attack. He was physically unable to farm and my younger brothers were too little to do it. I was released from my service commitment early and went back to Nebraska to farm and support the family.

I was ecstatic to be home. The army life had not been for me. It required discipline which I could not accept. It encouraged feeling good about being a soldier. This was post-Vietnam, and I did not, nor did many other people at that time, feel good about soldiers. I was glad to be out of the service and home. My friends, alcohol and drugs, were there too.

I had been home a few months when in desperation, I hid a large stash of pot in our house. (The mice were eating it in the barn!) I had never done this before, but I was not about to let the mice enjoy the pot more than I. The pot was in my gym bag in my closet at the back of the top shelf. It would only be there until my dad and I returned from town. You guessed it. My mother chose that day to follow her suspicions, and she found it. In a traumatic outburst, my parents kicked me out of the house and out of the family. This was the blow that broke my emotional back and my heart.

It was at this point that I began to fashion my personal emotional disaster in earnest. During the trauma of this incident, I became completely powerless over my emotions. My life would never again be the same. Before this incident, I felt insecure and fearful, but the fears would eventually go away. My emotions were not in control. I was. Afterwards, my fears controlled me.

I was very sad after my parents sent me on my way. Eventually, the sadness waned. Suddenly, I could not sleep! Sometimes for two, three, or four days in a row I would be unable to get any sleep! The sleep I did get would be disturbed and not restful.

My alcohol and drug abuse worsened. I behaved badly while under the influence and would be embarrassed and ashamed of myself. I just could not feel anything! There was nothing positive in my life. I had estranged myself from my parents, family, friends, and others. I was frightened of who I was and, sad to say, had created a living hell for myself. I felt helpless. I felt alone at the party.

I found EA through the grace of my Higher Power.

I crossed paths with the law due to my drinking behavior and ended up in jail. There were five transients in the cell with me. They passed six bowls of gruel to us and my cell mates made sure I did not get any. This incident caused me to do some real hard thinking on my state of affairs. My recovery began in that jail cell when I decided I had more worth than the situation I was in. I realized I needed to turn my life around. I pleaded guilty and entered a probation program.

My probationary program counselor confronted me. He asked me to set goals for my program. I laughed in rebellion and sarcasm. Amusingly, he noted for me that I was there because I had not been so smart, and he was smart enough to help people like me. Obviously, my attitude had not yet improved much! Grudgingly, I set one goal. I wanted to sleep normally again.

I went to A.A. as part of my probation. It just did not feel quite right to me.

In pursuit of my sleep goal, I eventually opened up to my probation counselor. I began to let all the emotions inside of me out. It was unbelievably wonderful. It was such a relief to let them out. It was like discovering a new world! I felt like an explorer uncovering wonderful treasures. So many of the mysteries of my life were explained by my feelings.

I realized my living problems — loneliness, insomnia, alcohol and drug abuse — were manifestations of my internal pain. I had low self-esteem and did not believe I was loved. After all, my parents had completely rejected me and did not love me. How could anyone love me? How could I even like myself?

Knowing I had emotional problems that needed fixing, I began to read self-help books. One of these books gave information on EA. I was immediately attracted to the idea of a twelve-step program for my emotions. It had always impressed me that A.A. had helped a million alcoholics recover from alcoholism. This gave me confidence the Twelve Steps worked and could work for me.

I attended my first EA meeting in the fall of 1976. I have been *home* ever since.

The meetings were fabulous! We actually talked about feelings without embarrassment. We talked about our attitudes and how to change ourselves and our lives for the better. I met wonderful people who accepted me as I was and accepted my struggles to understand what I needed to do to achieve emotional health.

Step One came easily to me. I could not sleep, and I knew my problems had an emotional basis. If I could control my emotions, then I would be sleeping. I had managed my life all those years, and where did I end up? In *jail!* Yes, I was powerless and life was unmanageable.

Step Two is my favorite step. I have found it to be the core to my health, happiness, and success in life. At first, my Higher Power was the gut feeling I had discovered in counseling. It has evolved to an understanding of the faith I need to be one with myself, secure with myself, and tolerant and patient with the world I live in.

Step Three has been the most difficult for me. I have found it is difficult because I lack faith. If I lack faith in a situation, I revert to putting myself in control. When I believe everything is going to be okay in my Higher Power's care, I give up control to my Higher Power. In the beginning, I had so many problems because I had so little wisdom and faith. I have recovered much of my emotional health now because I have been given wisdom and faith by my Higher Power through working the EA program, through the wonderful people in the program, and through my other life experiences.

Steps Four and Five have been wonderful! Getting rid of the baggage has helped me recognize my inner goodness. They have helped me know who I really am. I believe these steps must be completed to really work the program.

Steps Six and Seven have helped me develop the openness and willingness to change. I have learned I need not fear change. My Higher Power always has wonderful things planned for me. My relationship with my Higher Power has also deepened with my increased humility and communication.

Steps Eight and Nine cleared away so much baggage for me. Baggage that was the source of much embarrassment and shame. They also brought about healing. Not only were relationships which were important to me restored, but my relationship with myself has been healed.

Step Ten has kept me honest and kept my storage room of negative emotions empty. This step has been a great source of growth for me.

Step Eleven has brought me guidance and strength, the guidance and strength to know myself and make healthy decisions. I believe we make many decisions everyday, and only with spiritual guidance can I stay on the healthy path. Working this step also has deepened my oneness with myself and my Higher Power.

Step Twelve has been so rewarding and fun! I get great pleasure out of helping EA. I really end up helping myself. Doing for others helps me get and stay emotionally healthy. It seems each day in the program my spirituality spreads in the other affairs of my life. Using the program principles, my marriage and family, church, work, and other activities have healed and are for the most part successful.

EA's Twelve Steps have given me so many blessings! I have been in the EA program so long it would just take too long to describe them all and how they came about. However, I do want to briefly describe the most important ones.

I can sleep! Generally, I get six hours of sleep and sometimes more. It makes life a lot easier to live and is more enjoyable when I am rested.

No more alcohol or drugs! I was not chemically dependent because when my emotional health was restored my alcohol and drug abuse ended. I decided on my own, however, to end my use on principles of health.

I have normal feelings and express them now. I feel sadness and joy, hurt and anger, fear and happiness. I am alive and being me!

I have mended my relationships with my family and friends, at least as much as they can be mended. They are who they are, and I cannot change them. I have learned to appreciate this and to be satisfied with the way these relationships have to be for me to stay emotionally healthy.

I completed college and have a successful career.

I am a married man. In fact I have been married twice! EA helped me leave my first marriage which was without the spiritual love needed in a marriage and enter into one which does. We have two wonderful daughters and our own son. I believe I am a loving and supportive father.

I have self-esteem! Not all the time, mind you. However, most of the time I feel pretty good about who I am and who I have become.

I love. I love myself, my family, my EA friends, other friends, and life with all its mystery and wonder.

Finally, and most important, I have a living and loving relationship with my Higher Power – who has given me myself back, who has helped me, and who has given me so many blessings.

I would be the first to admit my life is not all roses and happiness. In fact, there are a lot of times it is just the opposite. I believe my somewhat fickle trust and faith in my Higher Power is the source of my recurring pain. It is a spiritual disease not to trust and believe. I work the EA program each day with the goal of becoming a person of even greater faith. I know every gain in faith I make will give greater emotional health, greater happiness, and more success.

As we say in the EA program, it will take me the rest of my life to become what I am supposed to be. My life has gone from a mess to a success! My life after I found EA is a wonderful blessing! It is a wonderful way of life given to anyone who works the Twelve Steps of Emotions Anonymous.

Thank you Higher Power! Thank you for everything!

MY ACCIDENTAL BLESSING

Agnes

My life was unmanageable. I was unhappy, lonely, and didn't have friends. I felt life was useless and just dragged on and on with no purpose other than survival. And survival for what?

One Friday night in July of 1978, I entered a church basement and heard some strange things like: "Turn it over," "Higher Power," "You are not alone," and "Keep coming back." This was my first twelve-step meeting, an OA meeting. Six months later I was to find EA. I keep coming back, and now I am no longer lonely and unhappy, I have friends, and my life has a purpose. I am on a journey of recovery which has given me the most exciting, adventuresome, fulfilling life I could have ever dreamed of having.

I was born the seventh and youngest child in a family with four brothers and two sisters. My mother was a paranoid schizophrenic, and we never had an understandable conversation. My father was physically abusive to some of us, and emotionally abusive to all. Mostly my memories of the family are complete emotional abandonment from our parents which we unconsciously carried over to each other. I do not remember any birthdays being celebrated, any Christmas tree with decorations, or any Christmas presents. We never had company, and my young friends knew better than to knock on our door. They would hear my mother scream at them to go away. I never talked about what was going on to anyone, and I lied about Christmas saying I had received many gifts. Most of all I remember an atmosphere of shame, loneliness, and isolation from each other with flare-ups of anger and violence. My family was like nine people in prison, each in our own cell. We could see each other, but we seldom looked at each other. We never shared our pain, shame, tears, or thoughts. Eventually we each left home. We opened our cell door and walked out, but we really carried our prison with us. At the age of sixteen I fled three hundred miles away to this unknown city of Chicago and survived. That's all I could do, survive. I was unbearably lonely but knew it was better than the hell I had left.

I learned how to get a job — lie about my age. I kept a job for a while, then I would oversleep and have to start over again drifting from job to job. I knew nothing about living, about relationships, feelings, trust, love, hope, spirituality, and all the things I now know make life worthwhile.

When I walked into that OA meeting in the church basement in 1978, and they said, "Give your food over to a God of your understanding," and "Keep coming back," I thought they were nuts — but nice nuts. I had nothing to do on Friday nights, so I came back.

There was a lady at this meeting who was very kind to me, and she offered to take me to an EA meeting. I didn't think there was anything wrong with me in that way, but she persisted. Feelings, emotions, anger, sadness — I had stuffed these down all my life. What to do? At EA I learned I wasn't alone. Other people had the same fears, distrust, etc.

There was a man who came to this EA meeting who said, "Do the very thing that you are afraid to do." He would say that several times at every meeting. Whenever I was afraid to do something new in the program like a step, a new behavior, or a new attitude, I would think of him and do it.

My journey in the program has been an onward journey of listening, reading, attending meetings, and working the steps. At first I didn't get a sponsor because I couldn't ask for help, but help was there as I just absorbed everything.

Step Three required me to put aside my lack of trust in God and just surrender and see what would happen. I followed what other people in the program did and said. I turned my life and will over to my Higher Power because under my power my life was worthless. Why not just be willing to have a Higher Power be in charge? I now do this on a daily basis by using the Third-Step Prayer.

Step Four was the most painful. I had to go all alone back to the pain of my childhood and put the pen to tear-stained paper until I was finished writing my resentments, my fears, and my story. I wrote about the resentments I had for my parents because they couldn't take care of me, the resentments of some of my brothers and sisters whom I thought could have helped me, the subsequent behavior of mine to get even with them, and my own destructive, passive-aggressive behavior toward them.

Then I did the most fearful thing I have ever done in my life. I asked a person in the program to hear my fifth step. I remembered that man who said, "Do the very thing you are afraid to do," and I asked my friend. She listened to me. She didn't criticize, judge, or berate me. She mirrored to me acceptance and love. I felt so grateful to her, to God, and to this program. I went home a new person, feeling free from the bondage of self, and a part of the whole world. I am not alone any more! In retrospect, I see the writing of the fourth step as the beginning of knowing who I am and validating that in the fifth step.

It may sound like I zipped through these steps so fast and my life changed overnight. That's not how my life works! I did finish Steps One through Five the first year. As I became alive to my Higher Power, an intimate relationship developed. I *trusted* someone (God) for the very first time, and then I trusted some people. I got a sponsor and became a sponsor. A sponsor/sponsoree relationship is important in my life and in my program. Together I have been able to finish all of the steps.

About eleven years ago, or in my sixth year in the program, I started to take an alcoholism treatment counseling course at our local college. I did not intend to use this for employment but as continuing growth to find out who I was and who I am. There had been alcoholism in my family. During this time, my own childhood issues were bubbling up so much because of these studies that for the first time in my life I sought counseling with someone whom I watched do some family issue work. Little did I know what would come out of this work — that I was sexually abused by my father. I had suppressed this all my life. I must have cried for three solid months, not just about the sexual abuse, but also about the total emotional abandonment by my mother. As I write this today, I can still feel that total lack and know I will never get the love from my mother because she was incapable of responding. But with God's love, I know today little Agnes is loved, and I take care of that inner child because I am a beautiful child of God.

My therapy was quick and total, and I knew that I was and am recovering. Going to EA meetings and having their support was what got me through that painful time. The old maxim, "The truth shall set you free," is alive and well. The shame I had felt all my life and the secrets I couldn't tell, and those I suppressed so I couldn't remember, kept me in my own prison. Now I am free. Now I am not afraid to tell you who I am. I am not afraid to live and not afraid to die.

Speaking of fear, I would like to tell of some coincidences that happened to me which touch on Steps Six and Seven, having short-comings removed. In May of 1989, I had been depressed for a couple of months. That is not my norm. I had been struggling with "Who am I?" Who were my parents and their parents — genealogy? I felt so alone. There had not been any soul-searching with my brothers and sisters about our shared life as children because this was too shameful to talk about. One day in May, I was driving to my meeting depressed. I suddenly sang out loud "Lord, give me a loving heart; Lord, give me a loving heart." This came out of the blue — or was it the Higher Power? My depression was instantly lifted, life felt better. I shared that story at the meeting.

I did not have a day of depression after that, even though a very trying experience happened with my oldest brother who accused me of things I didn't do. After many tears, I wrote a letter to him of my forgiveness for him, and I told him I loved him. This power to forgive and tell him I loved him did not come from me, I assure you.

In June I went white water rafting in the Grand Canyon with a friend. I went to the EA convention in Sacramento, California and spent two weeks in Lake Tahoe and Reno. There I landed in the emergency room of the hospital with a serious sinus infection and exhaustion.

Back in Illinois on October 17, the same day as the San Francisco earthquake, I was involved in a car accident. I hit five teenagers who ran a red light. They saw me and I saw them. We both braked. They weren't hurt, but I was. In the hospital the next day, after many tests, doctors found a tumor the size of a tennis ball in my heart. They said it had to come out, it was a matter of life or death. Alone I shed a few tears and immediately my program kicked in. I am powerless over this — what can I do? I turned it over to my Higher Power. I knew I would be all right regardless if I lived or died. I will be okay! A peace came over me which I cannot describe. All went well. A few days later when I woke up the doctor said if I had not had this accident I would have had a massive heart attack and not lived to talk about it. Remember, just five months previously I had prayed for a loving heart! How God fine-tuned my miracle. If the two drivers had not seen each other and both braked, I'm sure I would have been dead.

The reason I am telling you this story is that Step Six tells me to be entirely ready to have God remove my character defect of an unloving heart. And Step Seven says "Humbly asked Him to remove my shortcomings." This was my *accidental blessing.* Watch out what you pray for! Fifteen months later I again had open heart surgery. I am truly blessed!

I have done the amends in Steps Eight and Nine. Every day I work Steps Ten, Eleven, and Twelve. My morning begins with the Serenity Prayer, the Third-Step Prayer, and a prayer of gratitude for all the things my God has given to me: this program, peace, friends, love and life, a family at home and at meetings, an adventuresome spirit, a passion for white water rafting, a job of living and laughing, a thirst for knowledge about people and relationships, balloons, teddy bears, hearts, sunshine, flowers, ducks floating on water, children giggling, games, life stories, and anybody and anything that grows and becomes what God intended. Each day I ask my Higher Power to help me *love with this new heart* that God has given me.

This program works when I work it. This is an easier and softer way to live. I no longer am afraid of people. I seldom miss my EA meetings, retreats, and conventions. I share my story gladly because my Higher Power wants me to share . . . and I keep coming back!

Food Was Only a Symptom

Mary

It was February and as usual, along with my birthday, I was mentally evaluating my past year. Had I lost weight? Had I accomplished all those goals I had set for myself? As usual the answers were *no*. Again I was telling myself what I should have done. And, as usual I was not feeling very good about myself.

I was most concerned about my weight. I just didn't understand why I couldn't stop eating! I knew how to lose weight, but I sure wasn't able to do it no matter how hard I tried. The kids would come home from school, and I would have a snack with them as we talked about their day. Then I would continue to snack until dinner, eat dinner, and continue to eat, a little of this and a little of that, until I went to bed. Actually, on a good day I wouldn't start in on the food until the kids came home. This behavior really baffled me. I knew I just couldn't put off doing something about it — after all I kept gaining weight.

Except for my weight problem, my life was wonderful. I was happily married with two healthy, smart kids, and a dog. My husband had a good job and was helpful and supportive. We owned a nice house. I was involved in school and community activities and had made a number of friends through these groups. I swam three days a week which had been my sanity break since the kids were babies, and I played tennis in the summer. What more could I want? Wasn't this the American dream? I was sure I would feel better about myself and be truly happy when I lost weight.

Actually I had always had a weight problem. I was a fat child, and the baby fat just never went away. I knew this was the source of all my unhappiness starting in school when the kids made fun of me. I knew

221

I would have been more popular, those seventh grade dance classes wouldn't have been so awful, and I wouldn't have been so self-conscious all through school and even as an adult if I had not been fat. Now my weight was getting way out of hand again.

That very week I saw a notice in the newspaper about an organization called Overeaters Anonymous. I knew I was desperate for help because *I called* for information. I avoided making phone calls; that was out of my comfort zone. My husband took care of most phone calls because of my fear.

I went to my first meeting a few days later. I arrived just on time so I wouldn't have to talk to anyone. I was very shy. It was very uncomfortable for me to talk to people I didn't know well, or, worse yet, didn't know at all. I was glad the chairs were arranged in rows so I could sit in the back and not be noticed. I kept my coat on because I didn't feel good about how I looked.

The meeting started with the Serenity Prayer. Prayers made me uncomfortable, but this one seemed to make some sense. I had no idea what serenity was, but accepting the things I could not change was a novel idea. I thought responsible adults were supposed to be able to change everything that wasn't going right in their lives. It had never occurred to me that those things or people I hadn't yet been able to change I could accept as they were! For many years whenever I said this prayer, I had to disregard the word *God* because it was too religious and made me uncomfortable. This prayer continues to show me when I need to accept, and when I need courage. I am always grateful for the serenity it brings me.

Those who spoke introduced themselves as *compulsive overeaters*. I had never heard this term, but I immediately understood. Of course, I was eating compulsively; it made perfect sense. I could easily admit I was powerless over food for it certainly was making my life unmanageable. "So tell me how to stop so I can get thin and be happy," I thought to myself.

People were asked to read. This struck fear in me because I had a reading problem and reading aloud brought back memories of school days when having to do this meant stumbling over most of the words. It brought back the shame and guilt I felt when the kids laughed at me. I remembered all those years when I thought I was stupid. Now I was an adult in control of my life, and I wasn't going to humiliate myself by reading anything aloud.

However, I was interested in what they were reading because I wanted to know how they lost weight. They read some steps and something called traditions. Most of it didn't make any sense to me. I did learn this group was an off-shoot of Alcoholics Anonymous. It is a good thing I didn't know that before I came because I would not have come. I knew alcoholics were no-good bums who could, if they wanted to, just stop drinking. I was soon to discover that my food problem was very similar to the drinking problem of alcoholics. My drug of choice was sugar, and when I started eating compulsively there was no way I could just stop. We read A.A.'s big book at those meetings, and I saw clearly how similar my illness was to that of the alcoholic. Today some of my best friends are recovering alcoholics.

Then they read something called *Just for Today*. Here was something written in plain English which contained some good ideas. "Just for today I will stop saying, 'If I had time.' I never will *find time* for anything. If I want time, I must take it." I was always saying, "If I had time." If I had time I would have all those goals done that I set for myself last year. If I had time I would do some fun things instead of working all the time. If I had time I would spend more time with the kids. On and on it went all day long in my mind. I felt guilty if I took time to do things other than those on my list. Now I had permission to just take the time. I still have trouble with this, but I now realize I am making the choice of what I do with my time. I can't blame anyone or anything else like I used to.

Some slogans were read. Everything seemed to be in lists of twelve. "Look for the good" really caught my attention. Was this possible? My parents had always pointed out all the bad things which could happen.

They looked back over most decisions saying, "What if we had done things differently?" or, "If only we had known." They had always been very critical. I never seemed to be able to please them. Even as an adult I was still trying to please them and being crushed when their comment would be, "Why didn't you do it this way?" I too spent much of my thinking looking at how I should have done things better or differently, criticizing myself and others for just about everything, and expecting bad things to happen to my family. I was relieved bad things weren't happening, but I certainly knew all the possibilities. I was a major worrier and lived in fear. I also was certain I couldn't handle any problems should they occur. Fortunately, I had a husband who would handle them for me.

As the leader shared her story, I was amazed at her openness and honesty, and I could relate to most of what she said. She talked about working those steps. I thought if she was sick enough to need to do all that, okay, but I only needed to lose weight. She also talked about coming to these meetings for the rest of her life. Boy, she must really be sick! I only planned to stick around until I was thin because I had more important things to do with my time. Then she asked for a leader for next week, and I realized this was a volunteer job. I sure admired her for leading, but I knew I would never be up in front of anyone talking this way about myself. I never shared any of my innermost thoughts with anyone, and I could see no reason to change.

I returned to that meeting for many weeks. I began to feel comfortable there because no one forced me to do anything I didn't want to do, and no one was there who I knew. My normal friends, those who didn't need this kind of help, knew me as a very together, confident, happy person. I was very good at covering up how insecure and fearful I was. No one was going to know my weaknesses.

My thinking began to change as I used these new ideas, but I wasn't making the progress I saw in others. I asked the people who had what I wanted what they were doing. Everyone said they were working the steps. I didn't want to hear that! However, I knew this was what I needed to do, but how? So week after week, I would go and decide to listen as if I were a newcomer. I would not become impatient and just half listen because they were repeating the same things once again. With this new attitude, I was surprised what I learned. I discovered this was not just an intellectual exercise. I had to go home and apply this to whatever was happening in my life.

I had a taste of serenity, and I wanted more. I took the ultimate risk — I got a sponsor! This was very frightening because I didn't want to be open with someone else. She did much of the talking, and most of it was about working the steps. We talked about the idea of a power greater than myself. She pointed out ways she was applying these steps to her life. I was beginning to be honest and open with one other person. In some really powerless situations I had turned to a Higher Power and was *amazed* when this worked. I was even doing this once in a while just to see what would happen. I was eating less compulsively, and I was losing weight. I finally wanted to do Steps Four and Five, those which involved the personal inventory. I was excited about the progress I was making!

Then our family moved from Michigan to Arizona. I focused on looking for the good and turning over all the fearful situations to my Higher Power. I really hoped I could find another OA group. What I found was a whole new twelve-step program.

At this point in my recovery I had done Steps Four and Five and had changed because of it. I was doing Step One — I was getting good at realizing situations in which I was powerless, and not just ones involving food. Anytime my life became unmanageable I would look to see what it was I was trying to control instead of accept. I also was doing the tenth-step inventory most nights. I would review my day, looking for the good, and see how I might use more of this new knowledge in the next day. Only out of necessity had I dabbled with the Higher Power stuff in Steps Two, Three, and Eleven. However, the rest of the steps just didn't make sense!

I was sharing with a new OA friend about my frustration with the steps. She loaned me a book which had helped her. The book was called *Emotions Anonymous*. I read the chapter on the steps and found it to be a great help. I didn't read much else in the book because, of course, I didn't have any emotional problems.

A family friend from Michigan came to visit. She had been a once or twice a year visitor to our home since college days, and she was the only person in my life with whom I had ever shared very much. I showed her this book when she noticed changes in me and was interested in how I was doing it. She read a lot more of the book than I had, and I was surprised how much interest she had in it. We decided to attend an EA meeting while she was visiting.

At the EA meeting everyone said they were powerless over their emotions. I didn't know what emotions were, let alone what it meant to be powerless over them, but when it was my turn I said the same thing. There were many similarities here with the OA meetings. I felt very comfortable, and I knew I wanted to go back. My friend returned home to find her own EA group.

After my next EA meeting, I wanted to know what emotions were. I looked it up in the dictionary, and even then, I wasn't sure what it meant. "Emotion: any strong feeling, as joy, sorrow, love, hate, arising subjectively rather than through conscious mental effort. Syn. feeling." I began to make a list of the different emotions.

Then the light went on! I saw the connection. I didn't show emotions. I had suppressed them so often that I couldn't even identify them. My parents never showed emotions. I had learned early and well that we didn't do this. I must have also learned at an early age that food would suppress any emotion or replace whatever emotional need I might have. When I was angry I would eat; when I was fearful I would eat. I would eat when I was frustrated or worried, into self-pity, resentful, sad, or happy. I would eat when I was being a perfectionist, when I compared myself to others, when I had low self-esteem, and when I didn't feel successful. Any feeling I had could cause me to eat. No wonder food was such a problem! Emotions were the trigger to my compulsive overeating.

I attended EA meetings to hear people describe emotions so I could identify my own. Then I would begin to ask myself throughout the day, "What was I feeling?" For a long time, I had no idea. I decided to quit OA because I was not growing there, and I was tired of focusing on the food. Food was only a symptom of being out of touch with my emotions. I decided to label my compulsive overeating as a character defect and to use the steps to get rid of it as I had other character defects. I found myself less compulsive with food, and I was losing weight.

As I began to understand myself as a person with emotions, to recognize and label them, and to not suppress them with food, the pendulum began to swing the other way. My emotions were right at the surface and this made me uncomfortable. Sometimes an emotion would suddenly erupt, and I really understood being powerless. However, this was a necessary part of my recovery. It was no longer acceptable for me to use food to protect myself from my own emotions. I had all of the Twelve Steps to use, and, out of necessity once again, I began to apply them to each emotional reaction. I was excited about my progress, and I was losing weight.

It is now three moves later, and I am back in Michigan. We have a different dog. The kids are graduating from college. I have been divorced for over five years, partly because we grew apart, but mostly because I worked this twelve-step program and allowed myself to get in touch with my emotions. I found out who I really am, and the marriage became one which I had to leave. I do not use food as I once did. I recognize when I eat compulsively and look for what the real problem is. I now use food as a red flag telling me I need to take care of myself emotionally. My happiness and self-image no longer depend on me being thin.

I am not the judgmental, critical, unhappy person I was at my first meeting. I can be open and honest with myself and others. I am comfortable talking to people, and I no longer want to hide in the back of the room. I can cry and know it is okay. Fears no longer have the control they once did. I no longer set such unrealistic goals and judge myself as a failure when they are not met.

I believe the key to my recovery has been my spiritual growth. It was a tremendous struggle for me because I did not want to do all those God steps. Do you know how hard it is to go up stairs with half of the steps missing? Today I have a very close relationship with God, who is now my Higher Power. I expect miracles, and I am able to see the small ones as well as the big ones.

I was a member of OA for five years. My Higher Power knew I needed OA knowledge before I would be ready to understand that my true problem was powerlessness over my emotions. I have been a member of EA for over ten years. I have learned that working this program will not guarantee a perfectly happy life. However, it will provide the way to meet any life challenge successfully, especially if I am willing to share myself with others.

PART III

Tools for Recovery

Helpful Concepts

1. We come to EA to learn how to live a new way of life through the twelve-step program of Emotions Anonymous which consists of Twelve Steps, Twelve Traditions, concepts, the Serenity Prayer, slogans, Just for Todays, EA literature, weekly meetings, telephone and personal contacts, and living the program one day at a time. We do not come for another person — we come to help ourselves and to share our experiences, strength, and hope with others.

2. We are experts only on our own stories, how we try to live the program, how the program works for us, and what EA has done for us. No one speaks for Emotions Anonymous as a whole.

3. We respect anonymity — no questions are asked. We aim for an atmosphere of love and acceptance. We do not care who you are or what you have done. You are welcome.

4. We do not judge; we do not criticize; we do not argue. We do not give advice regarding personal or family affairs.

5. EA is not a sounding board for continually reviewing our miseries, but a way to learn to detach ourselves from them. Part of our serenity comes from being able to live at peace with unsolved problems.

6. We never discuss religion, politics, national or international issues, or other belief systems or policies. EA has no opinion on outside issues.

7. Emotions Anonymous is a spiritual program, not a religious program. We do not advocate any particular belief system.

8. The steps suggest a belief in a Power greater than ourselves. This can be human love, a force for good, the group, nature, the universe, God, or any entity a member chooses as a personal Higher Power.

9. We utilize the program — we do not analyze it. Understanding comes with experience. Each day we apply some part of the program to our personal lives.

10. We have not found it helpful to place labels on any degree of illness or health. We may have different symptoms, but the underlying emotions are the same or similar. We discover we are not unique in our difficulties and illnesses.

11. Each person is entitled to his or her own opinions and may express them at a meeting within the guidelines of EA. We are all equal — no one is more important than another.

12. Part of the beauty and wonder of the EA program is that at meetings we can say anything and know it stays there. Anything we hear at a meeting, on the telephone, or from another member is confidential and is not to be repeated to anyone — EA members, mates, families, relatives or friends.

Just for Today The Choice Is Mine

1. *Just for today* I will try to live through this day only, not tackling all of my problems at once. I can do something at this moment that would discourage me if I had to continue it for a lifetime.

2. *Just for today* I will try to be happy, realizing my happiness does not depend on what others do or say or what happens around me. Happiness is a result of being at peace with myself.

3. *Just for today* I will try to adjust myself to what is and not force everything to adjust to my own desires. I will accept my family, my friends, my business, my circumstances as they come.

4. *Just for today* I will take care of my physical health; I will exercise my mind; I will read something spiritual.

5. *Just for today* I will do somebody a good turn and not get found out. If anyone knows of it, it will not count. I will do at least one thing I don't want to do, and I will perform some small act of love for my neighbor.

6. *Just for today* I will try to go out of my way to be kind to someone I meet. I will be considerate, talk low, and look as good as I can. I will not engage in unnecessary criticism or finding fault, nor try to improve or regulate anybody except myself.

7. *Just for today* I will have a program. I may not follow it exactly, but I will have it. I will save myself from two pests—hurry and indecision.

8. *Just for today* I will stop saying, "If I had time." I never will find time for anything. If I want time, I must take it.

9. *Just for today* I will have a quiet time of meditation wherein I shall think of my Higher Power, of myself, and of my neighbor. I shall relax and seek truth.

10. *Just for today* I shall be unafraid. Particularly, I shall be unafraid to be happy, to enjoy what is good, what is beautiful, and what is lovely in life.

11. *Just for today* I will not compare myself with others. I will accept myself and live to the best of my ability.

12. *Just for today* I choose to believe that I can live this one day.

Slogans We Use

Let go and let God.

You are not alone.

One day at a time.

Live and let live.

First things first.

Look for the good.

By the grace of God.

Know yourself — be honest.

This too shall pass.

I need people.

Keep it simple.

I have a choice.

The Twelve Traditions

1. Our common welfare should come first; personal recovery depends on EA unity.

2. For our group purpose there is but one ultimate authority a loving God as He may express Himself in our group conscience. Our leaders are but trusted servants; they do not govern.

3. The only requirement for EA membership is a desire to become well emotionally.

4. Each group should be autonomous except in matters affecting other groups or EA as a whole.

5. Each group has but one primary purpose to carry its message to the person who still suffers from emotional problems.

6. An EA group ought never endorse, finance or lend the EA name to any related facility or outside enterprise, lest problems of money, property and prestige divert us from our primary purpose.

7. Every EA group ought to be fully self-supporting, declining outside contributions.

8. Emotions Anonymous should remain forever non-professional, but our service centers may employ special workers.

9. EA, as such, ought never be organized; but we may create service boards or committees directly responsible to those they serve.

10. Emotions Anonymous has no opinion on outside issues; hence, the EA name ought never be drawn into public controversy.

11. Our public relations policy is based on attraction rather than promotion; we need always maintain personal anonymity at the level of press, radio and films.

12. Anonymity is the spiritual foundation of our traditions, ever reminding us to place principles before personalities.

The Twelve Traditions reprinted for adaptation with permission of Alcoholics Anonymous World Services Inc. 1939, 1955, 1976.

The Twelve Steps

1. We admitted we were powerless over our emotions that our lives had become unmanageable.

2. Came to believe that a Power greater than ourselves could restore us to sanity.

3. Made a decision to turn our will and our lives over to the care of God *as we understood Him.*

4. Made a searching and fearless moral inventory of ourselves.

5. Admitted to God, to ourselves and to another human being the exact nature of our wrongs.

6. Were entirely ready to have God remove all these defects of character.

7. Humbly asked Him to remove our shortcomings.

8. Made a list of all persons we had harmed and became willing to make amends to them all.

9. Made direct amends to such people wherever possible, except when to do so would injure them or others.

10. Continued to take personal inventory and when we were wrong promptly admitted it.

11. Sought through prayer and meditation to improve our conscious contact with God *as we understood Him,* praying only for knowledge of His will for us and the power to carry that out.

12. Having had a spiritual awakening as the result of these steps, we tried to carry this message and to practice these principles in all our affairs.

THE TWELVE PROMISES

1. We realize a new freedom and happiness.

2. We do not regret the past or wish to shut the door on it.

3. We comprehend the word serenity, and we know peace of mind.

4. No matter how far down the scale we have gone, we see how our experience can benefit others.

5. The feelings of uselessness and self-pity lessen.

6. We have less concern about self and gain interest in others.

7. Self-seeking slips away.

8. Our whole attitude and outlook upon life changes.

9. Our relationships with other people improve.

10. We intuitively know how to handle situations which used to baffle us.

11. We acquire a feeling of security within ourselves.

12. We realize that God is doing for us what we could not do ourselves.

These may seem like extravagant promises, but they are not. They are being fulfilled among us, sometimes quickly, sometimes slowly.

How to Contact Emotions Anonymous

We invite you to attend our meetings and hope you will join us. You may find a phone number for Emotions Anonymous in your local phone book, in the support group listings in newspapers, or from community referral agencies.

You may also write Emotions Anonymous, International Service Center, P.O. Box 4245, St. Paul, MN 55104, for assistance in locating the nearest EA group. The International Service Center can also be reached by phone at (651) 647-9712, fax at (651) 647-1593, or by e-mail at generalinfo@emotionsanonymous.org. Our web site located at www.emotionsanonymous.org always has current meeting information.

If there is no group in your area, our staff will be happy to send you information on starting one. They will also answer any question you may have about EA.

Emotions Anonymous has many pieces of literature to guide you in your recovery. For a listing and description of what EA has available, you may request our catalog of materials from the International Service Center.

INDEX

A

AA. *See* Alcoholics Anonymous
acceptance
    vs. apathy, 49-50
    by group members, 97-98, 111, 172
        and hugs, 122, 131-132
        as unconditional, 27-28, 93, 107, 127, 155-156
    of ourselves, 49-50, 133, 148, 186
        and emotionally ill, 156, 157
        and Step One, 190
        and Step Four, 147
        and Step Eight, 66
        when others accept us, 19
    by others, 19
    of others, 93, 133
    of the past, 107
accident-proneness, 43
advice, 231
Al-Anon, 7, 144
alcohol abuse, 96, 119-120, 125, 154, 180, 208-210
    by family members, 106
    and depression, 124, 141, 205
    and suicidal tendencies, 85, 124, 150
Alcoholics Anonymous (AA), 4, 23-24, 144, 211
    Emotions Anonymous and, 2, 8
amends, 27, 66-68, 156
    alternatives when direct amends are impossible, 70

apologies as, 68, 102

and changing our behavior, 67, 68, 70

to children, 145

and forgiveness, 67, 68, 69-70, 143

for gossip, 70

and guilt, 68, 69, 94, 143

and healing relationships, 177

keeping amends simple, 69

to ourselves, 69

and painful memories, 68

to parents, 93-94, 202

by paying back money, 102

reactions to, 69-70

resistance to making, 106

and taking responsibility, 68, 102

willingness to make, 67

American Public Health Association, 23

anger, 41, 43, 48, 118-119, 137, 189

to control others, 195

at EA members, 193, 194

expressing, 146

and guilt, 195

lessening of, 121-122

at oneself, 199

and pain, 195

and physical illness, 195-196

at spouse, 154

and suicidal tendencies, 120

suppressing, 122, 130, 135

anonymity, 2-3, 162-163, 231

anorexia, 106, 117

anxiety, 1, 16, 20, 43, 58, 154, 180, 184

and anger, 196

and depression, 158
and physical illness, 179
and schizophrenia, 95
apathy. See *passiveness*
apologies, 27, 68, 102
assertiveness, 173
assets, character. See character, assets of
attitudes, 15-17, 34-35
about being a woman, 113
negative thinking, 16, 56-57, 99
positive outlook, 16, 151

B

backsliding. *See* slips, emotional
belonging, feelings of, 19, 60, 122, 146
and shared experiences, 144, 164
blaming, 20, 44, 125, 173, 180, 185
oneself, 164
vs. taking responsibility, 67
Bob, Dr., 24
boredom, 16
bottom, emotional, 87, 106, 166, 176
reached several times, 155, 157
and turning to EA, 20, 21, 44
bulimia, 117
businessman's opinion of Emotions Anonymous, 37

C

Carrying the EA Message, 11
carrying the message, 79-81
CEA (Children's EA), 12
celibacy, 128
change, fear of, 30, 212

character
   assets of, 65
   balancing assets and defects, 147, 168
   defects of, 56-57, 61-62, 63, 65, 142, 156, 182-183 (*see also specific defects*)
chemical imbalance, 116, 145
child abuse
   mental, 106, 124, 149, 153, 215
   physical, 88-89, 118, 123, 149-150, 171, 215
   sexual, 106, 123, 150, 153, 164, 218
   and shame, 164
child within, 121, 218
Children's EA (CEA), 12
choice, 101, 106, 122, 128, 152, 160, 169, 198
codependency, 64, 95, 153, 159
commitment, 111, 160, 190, 202
comparisons, making, 147, 160, 168, 170, 177
compassion, 139-140
compulsive behavior, 16, 48, 222
concepts, twelve helpful, 231-232
confidence, 29, 51, 97, 186, 199
conflict, 13, 172, 173
control, 189
courage, 22, 52, 107
Creator. *See* God; Higher Power
criticism, 231
   of oneself, 147, 224
   of others, 43, 55, 224
crying, 166, 207
cynicism, 196

D
daydreaming, 20, 106

death, 136
defects of character. *See* character: defects of
denial, 126, 128
dependency, 16-17. *See also* codependency
    on a Higher Power, 64 (*see also* Higher Power)
    on others, 64
depression, 1, 16, 20, 21, 43, 137
    and alcohol abuse, 124, 205
    and anxiety, 158
    clinical, 128, 145
    description of, 105, 141, 184
    medication for, 204
    and physical illness, 145
    relapses of, 115-117
    and suicidal tendencies, 106, 113, 124, 145
despair, 16, 21
destructive behavior, 43
differentness. *See* uniqueness, feelings of
directory, world, 10
discontent, 196
distrust, 196. *See also* trust
doctors' opinions of Emotions Anonymous, 23-26, 134
"Don't compare," 147
drinking. *See* alcohol abuse
drug abuse, 96, 113, 119-120, 154, 180, 208-210. *See also* alcohol abuse
    and paranoia, 205
    and suicidal tendencies, 150

E

EA. *See* Emotions Anonymous
"Easy does it," 170, 186
eating disorders, 123, 135, 137, 221-222
    anorexia, 106, 117

bulimia, 117
and emotional illness, 226-227
egotism, 55
emotional bottom. *See* bottom, emotional
emotional illness, 13-15. *See also specific illness*; bottom, emotional
    analyzing of, 14
    awareness of, 17-18, 41, 42-43, 156, 157 (*see also* Step One)
    downward cycle of, 20-21, 113-114, 124-125, 158
    and eating disorders, 226-227
    gratitude for, 137-138, 182
    guilt about, 154
    inherited, 116
    physical illness and, 1-2, 14, 26, 42, 117, 171
    symptoms of, 1, 13-14, 16, 20-21, 42-43, 184-185, 196
    unrealistic goals and, 13-14
Emotions Anonymous (EA)
    Alcoholics Anonymous and, 2, 8
    anonymity in, 2-3, 162-163
    definition of, 1
    emblem, 11
    financial support for, 2
    format of meetings, 167-168
    gender-neutral language used by, 4
    history of, 7-12
    how to contact, 5, 240
    keep coming back, 110-111, 142, 194
    literature, 4, 10
    medallion, 11
    as non-professional, 3, 30
    outside issues and, 3, 231
    prison meetings, 120, 121
    professionals' opinions of, 23-37, 134
    spirituality of, 3, 24, 25-26, 32, 166-167, 196-197

starting a group, 146, 169, 177, 181, 182, 202

Emotions Anonymous book, 11, 131, 134, 145, 159, 172, 205, 226

emotions. *See also specific emotions*

  awareness of, 132-133, 136, 160

  expressing, 148, 156, 157, 207, 211

  identifying, 226-227

  as neither good nor bad, 54, 146

  and over-analyzing, 132

  suppressing, 121, 146, 159

    learned in childhood, 130, 135-136, 226

    and physical ailments, 185

energy, 174, 197

envy, 43, 163, 196

escape, 44, 153, 180, 199

excuses, 14, 20, 109

  for avoiding EA meetings, 112, 167, 169

expectations, unrealistic, 13-14, 114, 125, 128

F

failure

  definition of, 146

  fear of, 42

  feelings of, 21, 43, 54, 154, 157

faith, 22, 143, 211

  in a Higher Power, 45, 46, 47, 48, 165, 213

fatigue, 16

fear, 14, 16, 21, 41, 137, 188. *See also* panic

  of change, 30, 212

  of criticism, 125

  description of, 105

  of failure, 42

  of fear, 180

  about the future, 162

of God, 180-181
and guilt, 135
of involvement, 42
lessening of, 97
and the moral inventory, 55
phobias, 86
of rejection, 42, 147
of relapse, 159-160
and Step Eight, 66
and survival, 119
of talking at EA meetings, 191
fearlessness, 54
feelings. *See* emotions
fellowship. *See* belonging, feelings of
food. *See* eating disorders
forgiveness, 218
and making amends, 67, 68, 143
of oneself, 60, 66, 69-70, 156
of parents, 90

G
geese in flight, analogy of, 90-91
goals
and the daily inventory, 72
setting, 115, 143
unrealistic, 13-14, 165
God, 34, 45, 47, 52, 147. *See also* Higher Power
awareness of, 60
trust in, 106
"God of my understanding," 166
gossip, 70
gratitude, 22, 102, 122, 156
to a Higher Power, 117, 137-138, 148, 191, 219-220

to a sponsor, 206
greed, 43
growth, 19, 30, 34, 190, 191, 212
guilt, 16, 17, 20, 41, 128
    and anger, 195
    and fear, 135
    about illness, 154
    from incest, 164
    and making amends, 27, 68, 69, 94, 143
    and Step Four, 55, 58
    and Step Five, 147, 148

H

habits, 15
hallucinations, 204
Happiness Clubs, 12
hatred, 119, 120
healing. *See* recovery
help
    asking for, 122, 125, 139, 166
    awareness of need for, 110
Higher Power, 25-26, 40, 45-46, 172. *See also* Step Two;
Step Three; Step Five; Step Six; Step Seven; Step 11
    awareness of, 60
    belief in, 46-48, 100, 147
    definitions of, 3, 52, 114-115, 137, 147, 211, 232
    dependency on, 64
    developing a relationship with, 52, 173-174, 189, 212
    fear of, 180-181
    gender of, 4, 52
    gratitude to, 117, 137-138, 191, 219-220
    praying to, 74-75, 103, 142-143, 173-174
    surrender to, 18, 52, 76, 102, 111, 219

trust in, 48, 51, 106, 165, 182, 190, 213
    will of, 51, 76-77, 127, 173-174
homicidal tendencies, 16, 43
honesty, 18, 45, 128, 168, 189-190, 191, 203
hope, 19, 21, 45, 48, 114
hopelessness, 171
hospitalization, psychiatric, 154, 176-177
    inadequacy of, 106, 120, 139, 142
    shame about, 155
    usefulness of, 116, 136
hostility, 142. *See also* anger
hugs, 121, 122, 132
human mind, 15-17
humiliation, 63, 195
humility, 45, 63-64, 101-102, 212
    vs. humiliation, 63
hypochondria, 95, 188

I

identity, sense of, 61, 141, 144, 145, 147
"I have a choice," 106, 166
impatience, 43, 142, 195
inadequacy, feelings of, 42, 114, 164, 188, 207
independence, 186-187
indifference, 20, 196
"I need people," 151
inferiority, feelings of, 21, 164, 179, 207-208
inner child, 121, 218
insanity, 127. *See also* emotional illness
insecurity, 42, 198, 207
insomnia, 16, 43, 175-176, 209-210
interdependence, 17, 138
International Convention, EA, 12, 146

International Service Board of Trustees, 9
International Service Center, 4, 9-10, 240
International Services Bulletin, 10
intolerance, 43, 55, 128, 195. *See also* judgmental behavior and attitudes
introspection, 160
inventory, daily, 71-73, 102, 225. *See also* Step Ten
and realistic goals, 72
and self-awareness, 142
inventory, moral. *See* Step Four
inventory, spot check, 102
involvement, fear of, 42
irritability, 20, 43, 195
isolation, 28, 60, 109-110, 151, 171, 199, 215. *See also* loneliness

J
jail time, 119, 210
jealousy, 43, 96-97, 196
journal writing, 161, 172, 193, 203
judgmental behavior and attitudes, 43, 97, 128, 179, 185. *See also* intolerance
Just for Todays, 107, 133, 138, 174, 177, 181, 223, 233-234

K
kinship. *See* belonging, feelings of
"Know yourself—be honest," 128

L
Lasker Award, 23-24
lawyer's opinion of Emotions Anonymous, 36-37
LEA. See Loners EA
learning, 163
"Let go and let God,"! 152, 181
lethargy, 197. *See also* energy

letting go. See surrender
location, changes of, 20
loneliness, 16, 21, 41, 42, 60, 215. *See also* isolation
Loners EA (LEA), 12, 134, 145, 155,
"Look for the good," 174, 223
love, 22
    feeling deprived of, 136-137
    from group members, 97-98, 146, 189
    of oneself, 124, 127, 147, 148, 152, 183, 213
    from others, 19, 27, 127, 151
    of others, 103, 127, 151, 183
lying, 109

M

manic-depression, 139, 141-142
    medication for, 153, 154, 155, 156, 157, 185
manipulation of others, 14, 113-114
Marion F., 7, 9
marriage, 113-114
    abusive, 89-90
    alcohol abuse in, 154
    codependent, 95
    supportive, 167, 168-169, 201
martyrdom, 127
maturity, 103
medication, 182
    for chemical imbalance, 116
    for depression, 204, 139, 145
    for manic-depression, 154, 155, 156, 157, 185
meditation, 75-76, 77, 103, 111
mental illness. *See* emotional illness
mind, human, 15-17
ministers' opinions of Emotions Anonymous, 31-36

Minnesota Intergroup Association, 8
miracles, 48, 103
mistakes, humanness of making, 148
mood swings, 139, 141-142
morality, 55

N
needing others, 122, 151
negative thinking, 16, 56-57, 99
nervousness, 43
Neurotics Anonymous (NA), 7-8
nightmares, 106, 121

O
OA (Overeaters Anonymous), 216, 222-225
obsession, 16, 145
"One day at a time," 52
open-mindedness, 47, 48, 64
Overeaters Anonymous (OA), 216, 222-225
over-sensitivity, 168, 195

P
pain, 14, 116, 127, 184
    and anger, 195
    benefits of, 94
    of recovery, 19, 54, 117, 202
    and self-esteem, 173
    vs. suffering, 172
    suppressing, 156
panic, 16, 21, 43, 106, 202-203. *See also* fear
    and alcohol abuse, 180
    description of, 109-110
paranoia, 43, 204, 205

passiveness, 43, 125
  vs. acceptance, 49-50
patience, 57, 173, 195
people pleasing, 123, 125, 127, 144, 159, 171, 179, 224
perfectionism, 14, 17, 113, 130, 175, 189
  lessening of, 111, 133
  and Step Four, 53, 147
  and Step Six, 62
perspective, putting things into, 146
phobias, 86. *See also* fear
phoniness, 14, 43, 199
physical illness, 1-2, 14, 16, 26, 117, 171
power greater than ourselves. *See* Higher Power
powerlessness
  admitting, 44-45, 96, 100, 162, 194-195
  over changing ourselves, 19
  over emotions, 18, 41-44, 146, 198, 209
  over others, 42, 172, 185, 213
  symptoms of, 166
  as a tool, 97
prayer, 74-75, 77, 103, 142-143, 173-174, 206
prejudices, 55
pride, 58, 66, 122, 179, 199
principles before personalities, 168
prison, Emotions Anonymous meetings in, 120, 121
procrastination, 43, 62, 73, 197
progress rather than perfection, 97, 128
promiscuity. *See* sexual experiences
psychiatrists' opinions of Emotions Anonymous, 28-29
psychosomatic ailments, 1, 16, 20, 42, 179-180, 184-185
psychotherapy, 27, 145. *See also* therapy
purpose, finding, 127

R

recognition, by others, 140

recovery, 20

    as hard work, 160

    pain of, 19, 54, 117, 202

    as a process, 128, 160

    upward cycle of, 21-22

rejection, 42, 211

relationships, 20, 65-66. *See also* marriage

    and breaking ties with family, 152

    with children, 115, 146, 148

    family, 43, 123-124, 135-136, 215-216

    with father, 88-89, 106, 118-119, 218

    with mother, 89, 95, 149, 218

    with oneself, 212

    rebuilding, 90

    at work, 1, 43, 82, 93

religion, 52

    inadequacy of, 106, 114

    spirituality and, 3, 31-32, 166-167, 196-197

remorse, 16

resentment, 14, 42, 43, 128, 137, 189, 195

    toward coworkers, 55

    and fear, 56

    toward parents, 55-56, 217

    toward siblings, 136

responsibility, 15, 18, 22, 27, 65, 67, 101, 122

    and making amends, 68, 102

S

sadness, 20, 135, 209

sanity, 47, 48-49

sarcasm, 195

schizophrenia, 95, 204
self-centeredness, 14, 21, 42, 58, 66, 72-73
    denial of, 127
    lessening of, 51, 52, 57, 191
self-confidence. *See* confidence
self-denial, 42
self-esteem
    low, 42, 124, 128, 130-131, 163-164, 179, 210-211
    growth of, 69, 115, 198, 206, 213
    and pain, 173
self-help books and programs, 86, 172
self-indulgence, 97
self-pity, 14, 16, 43, 124, 196
    denial of, 56
    and helping others, 103
self-respect, 22, 122
self-will. *See* willpower
self-worth, 13-14, 16, 46-47, 165, 197
selfishness, 43, 55, 183, 195
Serenity Prayer, 50, 128, 138, 168, 182, 190, 222
serenity, 18, 22, 137, 173, 195, 205, 231
Service Center. *See* International Service Center
service. *See* twelfth-step work
setbacks. *See* slips, emotional
sexual abuse, 106, 123, 125, 150, 153, 218
    and shame, 164
    by spouse, 89
sexual experiences, 56, 125, 128
shame, 42, 128, 199, 215, 218
    and group therapy, 27-28
    about hospitalization, 155
    about illness, 109-110
    from incest, 164

and insecurity, 207

shared experience, 21, 32, 100, 160

and belonging, 144, 164

and carrying the message, 79-80

and similar problems, 30, 110-111

shortcomings, 63, 64-65, 148

shyness, 42, 114, 186, 208, 222

silence, 48, 196

sleep, excessive, 48, 199. *See also* insomnia

slips, emotional, 73, 81, 128, 159-160, 196

slogans, 151, 152, 181, 223, 235. *See also specific slogans*

sobriety, 128

spirituality, 14, 24, 25-26, 30, 155

awakening of, 78-79, 168, 195

religion and, 3, 31-32, 166-167, 196-197

sponsorship

being a sponsor, 129 217

having a sponsor, 93, 100, 132, 203, 205, 206, 217, 225

in Loners EA, 155

Step by Step booklet, 156

Step One, 157, 190, 206, 211, 225. *See also* powerlessness

Step Two, 18, 45-49, 142, 206, 211

Step Three, 18, 49-53, 100-101, 147, 206, 211, 216-217. *See also* surrender

Step Four, 53-57, 101, 106-107, 142, 147, 168, 212

and over-analyzing, 132

and painful memories, 135, 217

and perfectionism, 147

Step Five, 57-60, 101, 217

fear of taking, 147-148, 164, 212

fifth-step person, 59-60, 132, 168

Step Six, 61-62, 101, 212

Step Seven, 63-65, 101-102, 212

Step Eight, 65-68, 102, 212

Step Nine, 68-71, 102, 151, 212
Step Ten, 71-73, 102, 212. *See also* inventory, daily
Step Eleven, 74-77, 103, 212
Step Twelve, 78-82, 212. *See also* twelfth-step work
stress, 154, 156, 206
stubbornness, 186-187
suicidal tendencies, 16, 21, 43, 116, 119
   and alcohol/drug abuse, 85, 124, 150
   attempts, 85-86, 100, 150, 158, 198
   consequences of, 120, 164-165
   and depression, 106, 113, 124, 145
surrender, 100, 195
   to a Higher Power, 18, 102, 211, 216-217, 219, 225
      (*see also* Step Three)
   willingness to, 101
symptoms of emotional illness. See emotional illness: symptoms of

T

"Take what you like and leave the rest," 166
temper tantrums, 48
tension, 16
therapists, 27, 29-31
therapy, 121, 158
   inadequacy of, 99, 106, 114, 120, 172, 188, 204
   usefulness of, 116, 136, 145, 150-151, 167, 218
Thérèse of Lisieux, Saint, 138
"This too shall pass," 128, 141, 152, 181
thought patterns, 15-17. *See also* attitudes toward life
Today book, 11, 111, 172-173
tolerance, 57
trust, 172
   building, 94, 121, 151, 217
   in a Higher Power, 182, 190, 213

Trusted Servants Temporary Committee, 8-9
turning it over. See Step Three; surrender
twelfth-step work, 97. *See also* Step Twelve
    examples of, 80-81, 111, 129, 170, 190-191, 202, 203
    learning to share, 103
Twelve Concepts, 167-168
Twelve Promises, 70-71, 102, 128, 151
Twelve Steps, 39-40, 160. *See also specific steps (Step One, Step Two,* etc.)
    as goals, 2
    repeating, 107
    working in order, 94
Twelve Traditions, 8, 236-237

U
unipolar depressive, 176
uniqueness, feelings of, 14, 28, 42, 157, 164, 180, 182, 202
unmanageability of life, 42-44, 125, 137, 194. *See also* Step One

V
vanity, 195
violent behavior, 43. *See also* child abuse; sexual abuse
volunteering, 80-81, 111, 186

W
Walther L., 8
wholeness, 160
willingness, 47, 48, 62, 174
    to change, 125, 212
    to make amends, 67
    to surrender, 101
willpower, 50-51, 100, 146, 170, 190, 196
Wilson, Bill, 24
withdrawal from others, 16, 21, 43

worry, 16, 20, 43, 166, 224
wrongs
    admitting, 58, 59-60
    determining, 58-59

Y
"You are not alone," 106
Youth EA (YEA), 12

Index Compiled by Carol Roberts